FREEDOM
for Your
SOUL

TERRICA SIMS

ISBN 979-8-89130-141-2 (paperback)
ISBN 979-8-89130-142-9 (digital)

Christian Faith Publishing
832 Park Avenue
Meadville, PA 16335
www.christianfaithpublishing.com

Printed in the United States of America

To my forever beloved Blessing, my teacup chihuahua dog, which I had for fourteen years. Her kisses and tail wags filled my heart with joy and made my world complete. Her presence made my entire life sweeter. She would curl up on her heating pad right beside me, keeping me company during my entire writing process of this book. With her by my side, my good days were greater and my hard days were half as bad.

On October 1, 2023, she gained her wings and became my forever guardian angel. I am eternally grateful for the fourteen years that we shared, and I will always love her. Thank you, Blessing, for your unconditional love and joy that you brought me and our family.

Rest in love, Blessing Miracle Sims.

Finally, to my loving and amazing parents, Bishop JR Sims and Dr. Julia Sims, who never stopped believing in me, thank you for being there beside me every step of the way throughout this entire process. Your love, support, and prayers are greatly appreciated. Thank you both for being my greatest supporters. I could never pay you back for all you have done for me and our family! I love you both always and forever!

CONTENTS

Hello, my name is Terrica. First, I would like to thank you for being courageous enough to desire change and freedom in your life by taking the time to purchase and read my book! I am excited to go on this journey to freedom with you. This journey is not easy, but it is so worth it! I just trust and believe that God will not put more on you than you can bare and that he did not lead you here just to leave you. He will be with you throughout this entire process! Your relationship with God will only get stronger as you go through this life-changing process! Once God reveals to you what has been stealing your freedom, you will be on a forever track to dismantle the chains of bondage that try to tie you up and lock you down!

There will be things that you will face that will be challenging to deal with, but they will be necessary for your journey, so hang in there and don't let go until you are walking in your freedom. Just remember freedom ain't free! It will cost you something. Your freedom is contingent upon the faith and the work that you put in! The more you invest in it, the more you will experience it! The sacrifices that you make will pay off in the end when you reach your goal! I am so excited that you are starting your journey, and I can't wait to hear about how God freed you and how you became a new person! I know that he can, and I know that he will! Do you believe that for yourself? I hope you do because I believe it for you and I believe in you! You can do all things through Christ Jesus who strengthens you! Amen! Now, let's dive into this book together, and again, thank you!

I have been led by the Holy Spirit to write this book for myself and for people who may be experiencing some type of bondage in their lives and are seeking freedom from it. Freedom to experience life and the world around you the way that God had in mind for you before you became tied up in the mental, physical, and emotional chains of bondage. God has been very clear and has spoken directly to me concerning the publication of this book. I was prophesied to twice about completing it! Thank you, Bishop Ronnie L. Web and Bishop Marcus McIntosh, for the confirmed word of prophecy concerning the release of my first book and books to come! Your words gave me the green light that I needed to go and get this done!

These two men of God didn't know me and had no idea that I was writing. They confirmed that it had to be done expeditiously and that God would use it in a mighty way! These prophecies were delivered to me six months apart. They both blew me away as it was the first time I had ever been in a service with either of them. I know that they are true men of God because neither of them knew me or know me personally. Finally, neither of them had any prior knowledge that I was writing.

This book has been birth out of experiences that have orchestrated the continual triumph, freedom, and victory in my life. I believe that it serves as a door or even a portal to launch you into a place of freedom and liberation from the shackles that were created to hold you back from your freedom. It is not by happenstance that you are reading this book. God ordained it to call you up to a higher a place of liberation concerning your life and your legacy!

After experiencing the amazing liberation of God from the spirit of heaviness and bondage, I felt absolutely compelled to help as many people as I possibly could to experience what I felt when God released me. My goal in writing this book is to expose the entrapments and bondages that people are dealing with on a day-to-day basis. I hope it empowers those who have been enslaved and trapped by the enemy and even, sometimes, by their own actions. I also hope that it sets you on fire with a passion not only for your freedom, but also for the freedom of others that are around you, and that you will share your stories and testimonies of how you overcame and became free by standing up and facing the work that it takes to break free and stay free!

I pray that it inspires and empowers you to break off the chains of antiquated mindsets, mediocrity, opinions, traditions, expectations, procrastination, disappointments, trauma, and generational curses concerning your life! I also pray that it gives you the momentum to move into the dimensions that God has designed for you so you can walk with confidence into your God-given freedoms, rights, promises, privileges, and purpose! My final prayer is that the trajectory of your destiny is vividly revealed and that you take the necessary steps of faith and work to walk into your freedom forever!

INTRODUCTION

Where the Spirit of the Lord is there is liberty.

—2 Corinthians 3:17

Frozen and Trapped

After being snowed in for two weeks, I looked out of the window and saw the sun shining so big, bright, and beautifully upon my face. The warmth from the sun embraced my face like a big, warm hug from God. It reminded me of how amazing and powerful our God is and how he created all things.

I started looking around, and I saw the ice and snow that was once frozen, finally beginning to melt away. I could hear the frozen icicles starting to drip away. I took a deeper look at what was going on around me. My spiritual eyes saw the ice melting and the water-drops running down the icicles to small puddles that represented a world of freedom.

God revealed to me that each waterdrop represented anyone that had ever been trapped, but somehow and some way got loose, and started moving toward their destiny and freedom. No longer was it trapped in a frozen state. As the water-drop was running down the icicle toward its freedom, the path of the icicle was getting smaller and smaller. As the end of the icicle was approaching, the only thing that separated the waterdrop from its freedom was the sharp, pointy edge. The water-drop had no choice but to trust that this leap of faith was going to set the trajectory of the rest of its abundant life. That leap of faith from bondage to freedom that we all must take in our lives will always be scary. The fall is terrifying, and the landing will hurt, but we can't let that stop us.

World of Freedom

What will this small drop of water do in the big open waters of freedom? It wanted to be free for so long, but now, it doesn't know how to handle its freedom. The waterdrop is afraid in the big, dark uncharted waters of freedom, but the fear of uncertainty didn't stop its quest for its liberty. It knew deep down inside that there was a world of opportunity that was bigger and better ahead. The uncharted waters weren't enough to kill the hope of a better life! The waterdrop had no idea that it was actually jumping into living waters. Those living waters would serve as its teacher, guide, and as the Holy Spirit.

As I reflect on my life, I see so many similarities to these waterdrops. You, too, may have felt frozen or even trapped in something that you have outgrown, and it no longer serves you. You know that there is better and that you deserve better for yourself and your family. Maybe it's a job, home, career, friendship, marriage, or even a relationship that no longer serves you, and it is detrimental to you and your future. You are now faced with a decision. Will you stay in your comfort zone and remain miserable, or will you fight for your freedom of a bigger, brighter, better future? Oftentimes, we settle for the easiest road with the least resistance, and we give up on our dreams. We let life drag us day by day instead of letting our faith lead us. It is never God's desire for his people to feel trapped or enslaved. He said, "I come that they might have life and life more abundantly" (John 10:10). While you are reading and when you have completed this book, I want you to take time to reflect over your life and any area that you feel stuck or trapped in. Examine how you got there, and let's create a plan for you to escape to your new bigger, brighter, better future of freedom!

Prayer Time

Father, thank you for your spirit of liberation. Thank you for breaking us free from the chains of slavery and entrapment that are constantly trying to bind us and conform us to the things that are not of you and the things that are not good for us. Thank you for saving us from things that are not healthy or advantageous for our future and our legacy. Thank you for removing the scales from our eyes and exposing the plots, schemes, and disasters that are hidden and laying waiting to ambush us. Thank you for saving us even when we were unsalvageable and a wretch undone. Thank you for your saving grace and your freedom! Thank you for the victory over slavery and entrapment in my life.

In Jesus' name, I pray. Amen.

CHAPTER 1

Freedom through Obedience

"Obey God and leave the consequences to him."

—Dr. Charles Stanley

Facing My Reality

Oh my goodness! I just can't take it anymore! I'm so over it! I'm about to lose my mind! When will it end? These were the thoughts that went through my head as we entered into another day of the two-week snow apocalypse of 2021! During this blizzard, I felt so trapped physically and mentally. I didn't know what to do with myself. We couldn't do anything or go anywhere because we were snowed in, and all of this was also going on during a global pandemic!

I had just made the decision to resign from teaching. I was so lost and confused about my life and career. This quiet, isolated time made me come face-to-face with my reality. My situation wasn't looking good, and my future wasn't bright at all. I was in a very low place because it seemed as if my life was frozen in time, with none of my new goals accomplished. I felt like I was watching my life pass me by.

I had decided to expand my business by going to massage school so my business could become a full-service spa. We were supposed to start school in January, but the tentative start date had already passed, and I hadn't heard back from the school. I was in such limbo about the next phase in my life. I was broke as a joke and barely surviving off the last of my retirement and my credit card. There I was, approaching my fortieth birthday, still staying with my parents after being on my own since I graduated from high school. My new career hadn't taken off as I expected, and I had no choice but to be there with them. Staying with them wasn't a problem because I love and respect them so much. The problem was there seemed to be no way to get out of the rut that I was in.

Have you ever had some quiet time that forced you to face your true reality? Those moments will happen, and they are okay if you are walking out of those moments with a renewed sense of purpose like I did. My quiet time humbled me and frustrated me. It also set a fire under me to overcome my situation and improve my life by doing the work to break free from my rut!

Searching for an Answer and Miracle

I went to God in prayer about all of this, and I felt like the woman at the well as Jesus was revealing the details about her life to her. She went to the well for one thing, but Jesus addressed a deeper issue that she had going on. There I was, standing in the midst of my issues, thirsty and desperate, looking for an answer to my problems! I was looking for God to come through for me in one way, but he came in a whole different way. I felt like I needed a miracle to fix my problems. Instead of him giving me the miracle that I needed so badly, he told me to write this book. I was like, "Really, God, you want me to write a book? Why, God? What does the book have to do with what I have going on right now?" Little did I know that he was using my situation to prepare me for something that I could never foresee.

He was using my rut to draw me in closer to him. He reminded me that my situation was only temporary and that my life would serve as a testimony for others. I didn't know how and I didn't even know where to begin. All I knew was I didn't get the answer I wanted from him, but I still had to trust him and be obedient in order to be in the will of God. He was preparing me for the next level of my life, and I had no idea. It took me a long time to get it, but I now understand that those things weren't happening to me, but they actually were happening *for* me. The book was the miracle that I needed, but I just didn't know it at that time!

I was stuck on the problems that I was facing in that moment, and God was trying to provide a way for me and my future. I could hear God saying to me, "Just trust me, Terrica. Although it may seem like I'm not addressing your issues, please know that my ways are not your ways, and my thoughts are not your thoughts. I am Alpha and Omega, and I can see your beginning from the end." I could also hear my spirit bear witness to the word of God by reminding me that God has all the cattle on the hills and that he is my source, not my resource.

God's Provision

This situation reminded me of God telling Abraham to sacrifice his son Isaac. Abraham didn't understand why God was telling him to do this, but he still trusted God and laid his son on that altar. This would have been the ultimate sacrifice! Abraham knew that God would take care of him no matter what. The level of faith that it took to prepare for this sacrifice was unbelievable. Imagine God promising you that you would be the father of many nations and that you and your wife couldn't conceive. Then when God finally makes you a father at an old age, he turns around and ask you to give your son up as a sacrifice.

I know I probably would have lost my mind having to do something like this prior to me hearing Dr. Charles Stanley teachings on obeying God and leaving the consequences to him over and over again. This teaching has reminded me that with men, things are impossible, but with God, they are made possible (Matthew 19:26). When God asks me to do something that I feel like I can't do or it is outside of my ability, I just say okay and show up because I know that he is going to meet me there and show out on my behalf. Hallelujah! I have learned that when obedience seems nearly impossible, God is going to supply a ram in the bush. If God gives you a vision, you better believe that he has already supplied the provision to accomplish what he has asked you to do. All you have to do is simply show up with the right heart and attitude like Abraham.

The Blessing Behind Your Obedience

I struggled with God about this book, but he was a true gentleman as he waited for me to simply say yes and do what he was telling me to do. He knew the impact my obedience would have on my life and others. The miracles that we often need to free us from our current situations are on the other side of obedience. I didn't want to do it, but the constant reminders from the Holy Spirit wouldn't leave me alone. I finally began submitting to God concerning this assignment because I knew deep down inside, obedience is better than sacrifice although I had never written a book and I was nervous and already so busy trying to figure out a way to work my way out of my rut. While I was trying to figure it out, God was already working it out for me!

In my yes to God, I reflect on how God blessed Abraham for his yes. God said:

> I swear by myself declares the LORD that because you have done this and have not withheld your son, your only son, I will surely bless you and make your descendants as numerous as the stars in the sky and the sand on the seashore. Your descendants will take possession of the cities of their enemies and through your offspring all nations on Earth will be blessed because you have obeyed me. (Genesis 22:16–17)

Your yes to God's will will not only be a blessing to you, but it will also be a blessing to your family, friends, and others. My yes to writing this book will be a blessing to people all over the world. I am so happy that I said yes! Now, the question is, Will you say yes to God's will? Don't delay God's blessings another day! Say yes, and watch God bless your socks off!

Are you trying to figure something out right now? Are you mourning over something that you can't fix? Are you tired of trying to work it out? Are you ready to surrender your wants and desires for his will for your life? Do you trust and believe that he has his best in mind for you? My final question is, What are you waiting for? My suggestion for you is to do it! Do it now! Do it early, and do it often until it is complete, and watch God work a miracle in your life!

Reflecting Time

Let's take some time to reflect on this issue and develop a game plan for this area of your life!

1. How has or does the enemy try to use the chains of disobedience to try to enslave you?

____

____

____

____

____

2. Do you find it hard to trust and obey God? If yes, why?

____

____

____

____

____

3. Did it work well for you when you did it your way instead of God's way?

____

____

____

____

____

4. How have the chains of disobedience tried to ruin your life?

____

____

____

____

____

____

5. What's holding you back from obeying God?

____

____

____

____

____

6. List the advantages of obeying God concerning this.

____

____

____

____

____

7. List three ways you can start obeying God more.

____

____

____

____

____

8. List three ways you can start dismantling the chains of disobedience.

____

____

____

____

____

9. Are you willing to say yes to God and obey him?

____

____

____

____

____

____

10. What are you believing God for concerning this area of
    your life?

____

____

____

____

____

____

My Pledge

Today, I pledge to myself to never allow disobedience to enslave
me again. I will do my best to hear from God concerning difficult
issues that I may face. Once I get directions from God, I will follow
them even if I have some doubt because I know that he knows what's
best for me. I pledge to dismantle the chains of disobedience over my
life through obedience to God's word by faith.

Signature: ____

Prayer Time

Father God, thank you so much for giving me the strength to step
past the voices of fear that tried to cloud my mind by saying it won't
work for me. Thank you for giving me the courage to trust and obey
you one day at a time, no matter how my situation may look! Father,
I ask that you continue to give me the strength to overcome and break
free through obedience. Although you may ask me to do something
that is difficult, please always remind me that you have your best in
mind for me. Thank you for the victory over disobedience in my life.
    In Jesus' name, I pray. Amen!

CHAPTER 2

Freedom from Worrying

Do not worry about your life, what you will eat or what you will drink; nor about your body, what you will put on.

—Matthew 6:25

Let us not be weary in well doing, for in due season we shall reap if we do not lose heart.

—Galatians 6:9

It's Working for Me, Not Against Me

When you trust and obey God, you don't have to worry, but there will be times when worry slides right in. It happens to the best of us. I will start with my true authentic feelings concerning this topic. I am so sick of me worrying! My faith man inside of me is sick of me worrying too! Worrying gets you nowhere! Worrying is like sitting in a rocking chair—you are moving, but you are not going anywhere. Worrying causes you to stress. Stress has so many bad health implications and even causes death! Worrying gives you gray hair, acne, and causes weight gain. Ain't nobody got time for that! I need my skin to be clear, my hair to be on point, and my weight to be together as I represent the kingdom of God! How can I represent the kingdom of God when I am worrying? How can I show up for myself or my family every day if I am worrying all the time? Worrying implies that I do not trust God and I don't trust that he is working all things together for my good.

We all worry from time to time. We all face insecurities, and we all hate the feeling of uncertainty. On this journey of life, I have had to face so many challenges that were outside of my control. I just had to throw my hands up and say, "Lord, your will be done in my life because I can't do anything about it anyway." My faith man has constantly pulled me up from the valleys of worry that present themselves and the low places that try to bury me and keep me down. A lot of inconveniences that happen to us are really working for us, and we don't even know it until the end of the situation is revealed to us—and that's if it is ever revealed. Say this out loud: "It's not working against me; it is working for me." Yes, all the attacks, rumors, insults, bankruptcy, betrayals, storms, trials, and tribulations are working for your good!

Opportunities Disguised as Inconveniences

We have to change our perception of things and begin to see that obstacles are simply opportunities that are disguised as inconveniences. Those inconveniences will cause you to have to do a little more work. Don't miss your opportunity by running from the work that has been placed before you. Embrace the work, and work it until everything is complete. The work is what refines, conditions, and prepares us for the next level. If we put off the work, we are ultimately delaying the outcome of our situation. How we do the work before us matters too! We can't do the work with a bad attitude, period! The work is designed to prepare us or give us a different perception on the situation that we are facing. When we are presented with a challenge or a test and our response is not a response of faith, I can guarantee that we will face that test again. Passing these different tests advances you to the next level. If you fail the test, you cannot matriculate to your next level.

I am still human, and there are some things that I don't even go to God first about because I know that there will be challenging work that has to be done. Sometimes, I just try to figure things out on my own, but when they are not coming together the way I would like them to, I finally have to go to Aba Father, knowing that I should have gone to him first! It's sad that I have to exhaust all my resources before I'm willing to go to the source! I ought to be ashamed of myself, but I am only being honest. Surely I am not the only one that does this. Nevertheless, once I make up my mind to go to him, I have moved past the fear of what I believe God will tell me to do, and I gird up my loins with my faith for the road ahead.

Time, Talent, or Treasure

God's answers to my issues seem to always be a sacrifice or an exchange of either my time, talent, or treasure. Matthew 11:28, 30 says, "Come to me, all you who ye weary and burdened and I will give you rest. My yoke is easy, and my burden is light." The exchange with God will always be better than the work. This scripture is saying that "if you simply come, I will take your yoke and burdens, and I will exchange with you because my yoke is easier and my burden is lighter than yours." The sacrifice will be hard, but your harvest will be greater than your sacrifices. So don't be afraid to make a tough sacrifice now for greater later.

I remember when I was buying my house. I was living in Nashville, Tennessee, and I was only approved for a $100,000 loan. Well, if you know how expensive it is to live in Nashville, then you understand that I didn't have many options. My realtor and I rode around, viewing foreclosed homes every other Saturday for nine months because that was all I could afford. Frustration was an understatement! I finally told her that I was not a "fixer-upper" type of girl and that I could not flip a home by myself. I made the decision not to buy until I was approved for a larger line of credit.

Seedtime and Harvest

I went to God in prayer because I was so worried that I would never be able to purchase a home with such a small line of credit. I presented my requests, and I would thank him in advance! I would say, "God, I saw you do it for my sister and brother-in-law, so I know you can do it for me." My two requests were very big, but I served a bigger God. I told God that I wanted a brand-new home. I also told him that I wanted my mortgage to be less than my rent was. My rent was $530 per month. These were almost impossible requests, but I just believed that God could do anything but fail. God told me to increase my giving, and I was obedient. In addition to my tithes, I started giving an additional $100 per paycheck. Oh my goodness, I remember how hard that sacrifice was at that time! I had no idea that my sacrifice or seed would pay off like it did and is still doing till this day!

I remember it like it was yesterday. My realtor called me while I was in Arkansas at my family reunion. She said, "Terrica, I found a house for you that I believe that you would love."

I said, "Vivian, is it a foreclosure?" She said yes, and I said I was not interested. She proceeded to tell me that I had to get home as soon as possible because this was an incredible deal. I finally told her that I would come home to see it. The next week, as I am driving to see this home, I told God that I needed a green light—not a yellow, not a red. I needed a green light to know that it was what he wanted for me. I pulled up into the subdivision, and I was behind a red drop-top convertible with a license plate that said "Slam Dunk"! I knew then that it was going to be amazing, and it would be the answer to my prayers.

My Harvest Was Greater than My Sacrifice

I walked into a brand-new home that had been sitting on the market for three years since its previous owners walked away from it. They had gotten married and stayed in the house for only six months, then they got a divorce. They both walked away from it, and let the house get foreclosed on. When I walked into this house, I was blown away. It was better than anything I could have imagined. I asked my realtor how much they were asking for it. She looked at me and said $75,900. In total disbelief, my mouth dropped! I could not believe it! God had made a way for my little bitty $100,000 loan to work in Nashville, and I didn't even have to use all of it. He is a way maker, hallelujah! We offered $75,000, and they countered with $76,900. We took it.! My mortgage was less than my rent by $15, and I had a brand-new home! God gave me more than what I asked for. My harvest was greater than my sacrifice! Hallelujah! Thank you, God! I just got happy thinking about it again because he is faithful and he is going to take good care of his children.

The Overflow of Blessings

God wasn't finished blessing me for trusting and obeying him. I was blessed with a $5,000 first-time home buyer grant. I was also blessed with 10 percent of my realtor's commission, which was $800. Last but not least, when I signed my name for the purchase of the home, I already had $40,000 of equity in the home! God blew me away! He still wasn't finished blessing me.

A few years into my home, someone called me and told me that I could get a better interest rate if I refinanced my home. I said I'm okay with the interest rate that I have, which was 5 percent. She went on to say, "Do you have any student loans?" I knew that I had already paid half of my student loans, but I still owed $20,000. She told me that I could pull that amount out and pay off my student loans. I did just that! So not only did I get a brand-new home with a mortgage that was less than my rent. Not only did I get $5,800, but I also got my student loans paid off and a lower interest rate of 3.75 percent! I got all of this because of my obedience to increase my giving by $100 per paycheck. When God told me to do this, it was a huge sacrifice because I was hardly making enough money to do life with. I was worried about how I would make ends meet with the increase of my giving. This was a huge sacrifice for me, and I am still reaping a harvest from my seed and my sacrifice!

Today, I only owe $73,000, but my house has been appraised at $257,000! Won't he do it! Can I tell you that it is my first rental property, and I still make money off it every month! This all started because of what seemed impossible for me in my strength, nevertheless, I was reminded that "God's grace is sufficient, and his strength is made perfect in my weakness" (2 Corinthians 12:9)! When I get frustrated, I reflect on how God blew my mind away with this situation and how he can do it again for me in every area of my life! He will make a way out of no way! He is a waymaker, miracle worker, promise keeper, light in the darkness—my God, that is who he is.

Let Go, and Let God

One of my favorite artists of all time is PJ Morton, who wrote a song called "Let Go." The lyrics say:

> As soon as I stopped worrying
> Worrying how the story ends
> When I let go and I let God
> Let God have his way.
> That's when things start happening
> When I stopped looking at back then
> When I let go and I let God
> Let God have his way

There is nothing more freeing than when you finally release every issue that you are worried about over to Daddy God. It relieves so much pressure and stress that you put on yourself. Things aren't as tight, and you can move a little bit better. It feels like you were about to drown, and then you were finally able to make it to the top to breathe. Stop worrying about tomorrow, and take a sigh of relief. We may not know what tomorrow holds, but oh, we are so blessed to know who holds tomorrow! He holds the whole world in his hands. Rest in knowing that God is working it out for you if you don't give up!

Trusting that God has his best in mind for you through every situation will help you with your worrying. Knowing that he is working all things together for your good can also reassure you that you will come out better than you were before! If we really think about it, honestly, what can't God do? Do you think that he is pressed by the challenges that we face? Nothing is too hard for God! Does he love you? Absolutely! Will he take care of you? Absolutely! Will he perfect those things that concern you? Absolutely! Have you ever seen the righteous forsaken or his seed begging bread? If he clothe the lilies of the field, how much more will he do for you? So stop worrying and start trusting!

Even writing this book was worrisome for me, but I just did it and trusted that he would bless my efforts and bless others in the process! Just like God blessed me with my home when there seem to be no way! He gave me more than I could have ever asked for. He blessed me exceedingly and abundantly than I could have ever imagined! Who wouldn't serve a God like this?

Make Your Request Known

Remember that when you stop worrying and you present your request to God by prayer and petition with thanksgiving, God will give you the peace, which transcends all understanding, and it will guard your heart and mind in Christ Jesus. God wants to give you peace beyond your understanding and your worries! Peace is a promise to you. What a mighty God we serve! Hallelujah! I don't know about you, but I need me some peace at all times! Amen, and thank you, God, for being my Prince of Peace!

Finally, the famous song writer once said, "Don't worry, be happy." I know that it is easier said than done, but guess what? I believe in you! I know you can do it! Do you believe in yourself? Will you trust God when you can't trace him? Will you lean not onto your own understanding and lean on him? He is willing and able to honor your request. Start writing them down, and present them to him. He wants to bless you! If he did it for me, I know he can do it for you! Amen!

Reflecting Time

Let's take some time to reflect on this issue and develop a game plan for this area of your life!

1. How has or does the enemy try to use the chains of worrying to try to enslave you?

____

____

____

____

____

2. What are you worried about and why?

____

____

____

____

____

3. List and compare the advantages and disadvantages of worrying.

____

____

____

____

4. How have the chains of worrying tried to ruin your life?

____

____

____

____

____

5. What will it take for you to give it over to God and leave it at his feet?

____

____

____

____

____

____

6. List the advantages of worrying less and trusting God more concerning this.

____

____

____

____

____

____

7. List three ways you can start trusting God more.

____

____

____

____

____

8. List three ways you can start dismantling the chains of worrying.

____

____

____

____

____

9. Are you willing to say yes to God and trust him more?

____

____

____

____

10. What are you believing God for concerning this area of
    your life?

\
\
\
\
\
\

My Pledge

Today, I pledge to myself to never allow worrying to enslave me again. I will do my best to hear from God concerning different issues that I may face that cause me to worry. Once I get directions from God, I will let go and let God have his way, even if I have some doubt because I know that he knows what's best for me. I pledge to dismantle the chains of worrying over my life through trusting God's word and working by faith.

Signature: _______________________________________

Prayer Time

Thank you, Lord, for your peace! The peace of God, which transcends all understanding will guard my heart and my mind in Christ Jesus. Even in my insecurities, you secure me! Even when my anxiety tries to overtake me and throw me into an endless pit of worry, I will rest in you, for you are my refuge, my fortress, my God, in whom I trust. Thank you, Lord, that no matter what I face, you will perfect that which concerns me. God, give me the strength I need so I can lay all my worries and anxiety at your feet. I put my trust in you, and I rest in you! Thank you for the victory over the worrying in my life.

In Jesus' name, I pray. Amen!

CHAPTER 3

Freedom through Forgiveness

*If it is possible, as far as it depends on
you, live at peace with everyone.*

—Romans 12:18–19

Is Unforgiveness Your Slave Master

Unforgiveness is one of the biggest slave masters that keep us enslaved and trapped for years and decades. Some people even die with unforgiveness in their heart. It is so sad how people let this trick of the enemy tear up their lives! One of the hardest things you will ever have to do is forgive a family member or a friend who has wronged you. It's harder than forgiving someone you don't know because those people are not close to you and you don't have to be around them often. Offense and unforgiveness are used by the enemy as weapons of spiritual warfare that are designed to kill, steal, and destroy families and friendships. If we are not careful, it will do just that and more. If you let it get too far gone, it could possibly destroy you!

I remember as a kid, when things would happen with other kids, our teachers or our parents would bring us together and make us say, "I'm sorry," and the other kid would have to say, "It's okay." We didn't mean it. We were just going through the motions so we could continue to play. As we got older, we were taught that we had to be the bigger person and just forgive them, even if they never acknowledged the hurt that they caused. This would tear me up on the inside because they would just move on like it was nothing, and I would be trapped in those hurt emotions each time I saw them or had to relive those scenes in my head when I thought about them. I didn't know how to overcome those feelings. They would also have the audacity to tell me that I still needed to be cordial with the person that hurt me. I don't know about you, but that made me feel faker than a three dollar bill! I would be boiling that I had to speak to them, knowing that they did me wrong.

Forgiveness Isn't Just Lip Service

My forgiveness was only lip service. I would say that I forgave people, but I would just cut them off and never deal with them again if possible. That didn't work so well when someone I loved hurt me. I couldn't just cut them off. I still would have to see them from time to time and ignore the fact that they hurt me. My unforgiveness had me trapped up like I was in a stray jacket. Can you imagine feeling like you are trapped in a stray jacket—hot, uncomfortable, and tight? That is what would happen when I would see these people. I wouldn't be myself. I would be very uptight because their presence made me uncomfortable. It made me change who I was and what I did when I was around them. I didn't know how to handle these issues. Not being equipped or educated to deal with the severities and difficulties of these situations only victimized me even more.

One of the life-changing ways that I learned about forgiveness is when I wronged someone and I needed and wanted to be forgiven! I needed their grace to be extended toward me. This situation was one of the hardest things that I have ever been through! Offense broke up my relationship with my former church home, and it was killing me. The enemy uses hurt and offense to distract you and separate you from God's promises and his people.

Church Hurt

I will never forget the former single ministry pastor of our church who asked me to go on a date. We went to the mall, and we grabbed some food in the food court. One of the ladies from the single ministry, who happened to be one of the pastor's favorites, saw us and was acting very differently toward us. When I saw her after church the next day, I asked her why she was acting so weird. She said, "Let's ask him."

I called him, but he didn't answer. So I said, "Let's stop by his house."

He let us in to talk, but as we were talking, the conversation got very intense, and we soon found out that the two of us were not the only women that he was dating. We eventually left his home. Within two hours of getting home, I got a call from the assistant pastor saying that the senior pastor wanted to have a meeting with me. I called her and asked her if she told the senior pastor what happened. She told me, "No, but I did tell the assistant pastor." I was so upset because she was the only person who got upset and reacted in such an irate manner.

The pastor, his team, and I met, and it had the be the longest meeting that I had ever been in in my life. He let me know the reason why the guy was no longer the single's pastor and basically was trying to give me reasons to leave him alone. He didn't like that, and I knew that my time there was coming to an end. But it was a very intense meeting.

I left that meeting so upset because it just made things worse. After that meeting, I was hurt so I started asking some of the church members some thought-provoking questions about the ministry and its practices. My questions were relevant, but they came from a hurt place and were considered seeds of discord. Church leaders started calling me to meet with me for "dinner." I would always decline because I was hurt, and I knew why they wanted to meet with me. I didn't want to talk to anyone. I would go to church late and leave early to avoid conversations with people.

The assistant pastor finally saw me at choir rehearsal and told me that pastor wanted to meet with me. I left the choir rehearsal, and we met in his office. He told me that he could no longer cover me as a pastor because of me questioning the ministry's practices and sowing seeds of discord. I got my things and left. I was so hurt! Let me tell you. There is no hurt like a church hurt. I left that church so broken, lost, and confused. My spirit man was destroyed because that was the only family I had in Nashville at the time.

After the Hurt, There Is Healing for Your Soul

I started visiting another church called Oasis Worship Center, where Danny Chambers was the pastor. They were starting their new semester of life classes. I signed up for one called "The Bait of Satan." If you haven't read it, please do. That book changed my life forever concerning forgiveness and bondage in other areas of my life! While in this class, I asked God to forgive me, and I forgave myself for causing issues at the church with my questioning.

I thought I had forgiven the pastor who told me he couldn't cover me anymore. There I was, living my best life in my new church home, healing from the hurt and loving myself. Then out of nowhere, I saw the pastor's wife in the store. My heart started racing, and I could hardly talk. I went back to my life class teacher and told him about the encounter. He told me that those were signs of unresolved issues that needed to be fixed. I asked him why, and he told me, "You shouldn't have those types of reactions when you see someone." He showed me Romans 12:18–19, and it said, "If it is possible, as far as it depends on you, live at peace with everyone."

Then he asked me, "Do you have peace with them, or do you just think you have peace with them?" I knew then my peace wasn't complete and that I had to pursue peace and work hard to get it.

I typed up an email asking for forgiveness for my actions and telling him that I wanted to live peaceably with him and the church if possible. I asked others for his email address, and no one would give it to me. I was so upset because I had to go to the church and leave it with someone. I prayed about it, and I took a deep breath and drove up to the church. I left it with one of the members. Within ten minutes of me dropping it off, his secretary called me and said that pastor wanted to meet with me. I drove back to the church, and he and his wife welcomed me back like the prodigal daughter. I left that meeting with the forgiveness and peace that I needed from them. I would visit them from time to time, and they would welcome and love on me each time. Their forgiveness was like healing to my soul. It healed me and us. I was able to see and visit my old church family like old times. Their forgiveness truly taught me to give grace to others and allow room for error with people because no one is perfect.

Your freedom from unforgiveness will require consistent faith to overcome because offense is inevitable. It is not a one-step solution; forgiveness is a process that takes time and work. Faith without work is dead, so if you are not willing to do the work that is required for your freedom, you will be trapped forever. I could have given up when they wouldn't give me his email address, but I didn't. I fought through my fears and tears, and by faith, I drove up to the church with my heart beating outside of my chest. I put my pride and ego aside and fought for my peace! I wouldn't allow it to trap me any longer. Don't stay enslaved to offense and unforgiveness. Work hard by faith and fight for your freedom like I did!

Forgiveness Is Really a Trust Issue between You and God

As I have grown and matured, I have learned two crucial things about forgiveness. The first thing is that forgiveness is really a trust issue. When you truly forgive, you are telling God, "I don't know why this happened to me, but I trust you enough to forgive them, even if there is no apology or explanation." I used to wait and wait for people to explain why they did me a certain way. I learned that most people will not admit to wrongdoing. They have rationalized why they are right. They would rather sweep things under the rug and act like nothing ever happened. After realizing these things, I learned that I could no longer wait for their explanation to be free from their offense, and I had to just forgive and put it all in God's hands. Forgiveness is a seed that will always reap a good harvest!

Stop Demanding, and Let God Be God

The second crucial thing that I learned was forgiveness wasn't just for them, but more so for me and my peace! I had to understand that it wasn't letting them off the hook, but instead, it was taking me off police duty and letting God be God! Hallelujah! I no longer had to police people on how they treated me. I had to take my hands off it. They had to answer to God concerning me, and he doesn't play about his children. When I got this understanding, I was totally free! My freedom is no longer contingent upon their excuses or explanations! I am *free* with or without them! Forgiveness is a decision to offer grace instead of demanding justice (Gary Chapman).

Luke 17:1 warns us, and it says, "Offense will come." So just know that it's coming, one way or another. Don't be surprised when it does; just be prepared. James 1:2–4 says, "Count it all joy when you fall into various trials, knowing that the testing of your faith produces patience. But let the patience have its perfect work, that you may be perfect and complete, lacking nothing." These trials come to make us stronger, wiser, and better so that we are lacking nothing! When patience has its perfect work, we will come out as pure as gold!

It Is Working for Your Good

God has given us strategies on how to handle them, and none of these strategies are easy to do. They all involve trust in God, consistent faith, and work! The hardest thing is trusting God through the offense and believing that God is working all things together for your good! While I was going through this church hurt, God led me to my new church home that changed my life forever. I became an active member there eleven years after that. I grew so much spiritually! It worked out for my good in so many ways! The good that came behind my church hurt outweighed the pain I went through significantly! My life was improved and enhanced tremendously.

With the consistent and amazing teaching of Pastor Danny, I started understanding that my walk with God was not based upon rules on what I could or couldn't do, like I had been taught all of my life. Instead, it was about being in a relationship with him. Once I learned this concept, I was more concerned that I pleased God instead of breaking rules. God freed me from people! Once you are free from people, you really don't care what they think, and you begin to see who has been trying to keep you trapped in their systems and man-made rules. God freed me from all of that junk! John 8:36 says, "Who the Son set free is free indeed!" I am free, and you can be too! Everything you need is on the inside of you, and that's God! Don't forget that greater is he that is within you than he that is in the world! The greater one lives inside of you, and you can overcome anything because you are more than a conqueror!

Oasis Worship Centre was a spiritual oasis for me. It was so impactful that I named my spa business Oasis Beauty Bar LLC because I wanted it to be a life-giving place like Oasis church was to me!

Avoidance Doesn't Work

Not dealing with unforgiveness will keep you bound and enslaved to a person or thing for years because you aren't willing to deal with it. Stop choosing avoidance; it is not making the situation better. The choice is yours—will you do the work by faith to overcome the offense, or will you stay trapped in a very uncomfortable and tight stray jacket and chains called unforgiveness?

Forgiveness Is Mandatory; It Is Not Optional

The same grace and forgiveness that you need when you sin or make a terrible decision against someone else is the same grace and forgiveness that others need when they sin or make a terrible decision concerning you. As you extend grace and forgiveness, your heavenly Father will give the same to you according to Mathew 6:14–15: "When you forgive others, your heavenly Father will not withhold forgiveness from you. If you do not forgive others for their sins, your Father will not forgive your sins."

It is your responsibility to pursue reconciliation and peace through forgiveness and communication. After you have done your part, the rest is up to them. Matthew 5:23–24 says, "If you are offering your gift at the altar and there you remember that your brother and sister has something against you, leave your gift at the altar, and go be reconciled to them; then come and offer your gift." God is speaking and saying, "Go and make it right by doing your part before you bring any offering up to the altar for me."

Even if they wrong us, we are still responsible for pursuing peace with them. Matthew 18:15–16 says, "If your brother wrongs you, go and talk with him at once. If he listens to you, you have won him back as a brother." Being the bigger person can be tough for anyone. How they treat you is on them. How you respond is on you, and it is the determining factor if you will pass this test. Take care of your business, and trust the process. Please don't let unforgiveness trap and chain you up for years.

Revenge Is Not an Option

Our very human nature is to repay or get someone back for wronging us. We want them to hurt like they hurt us. When we take on the responsibility to get someone back, we are putting ourselves and others in harm's way. The old saying goes like this: "If you are going to dig one ditch, you better dig two because the first one might just be for you." The seeds of revenge never reap a harvest of peace. It only makes things worse for you and everyone that you are connected to. The people you love suffer when there are detrimental consequences to your vengeance.

I have not only seen this happen to other people, but my family and I have experienced this firsthand. My nephew's life was taken because someone was trying to get someone else back. This was a real big hit to our family. It was and is still such a sad situation for us as we continue to grieve his loss. Now, all we have are the memories of him. Before you take on repaying evil for evil, please consider your family and everyone that is connected to you.

Romans 12:19 tells us, "Do not take revenge, my dear friends, but leave room for God's wrath for it is written vengeance is mine; I will repay, saith the Lord." The scripture goes on to say that if your enemy is hungry, feed him. If your enemy is thirsty, give him drink for in doing so, you shall reap coals of fire on your enemy's head. Then we are instructed to not be overcome with evil but overcome evil with good (Romans 12: 20–21).

We have to stop playing the role of God and let God do what only he can do. Free yourself from trying to get revenge on someone, and let God handle it! He can do it way better than we can anyway. I think we get caught up in wanting to see people suffer how they saw us suffer. There will be times that you will never see what God has in store for those who hurt you. The Bible does give us some hope in Galatians 6:7 as it says, "Be not deceived; God is not mocked: for whatsoever a man soweth, that shall he also reap." So stop worrying your pretty little head off about getting them back. God has that covered, and it is laid out clearly here that it is taken care of!

For some of you who may say, "I just have to get them back for hurting me and my family like this," I want you to know that you are not dealing with a revenge issue; you are dealing with a trust issue. Your trust issue is with God! You don't trust him to do what he said he was going to do. Now I want to know why you don't trust God. Are you used to doing everything by yourself, and you find it hard to depend on others? He is a God that cannot lie. That is his word, and he stands on it. While we are pulling our hair out stressed about it, God has already perfected everything for you. He is a God of details, and he has not forgotten you or your situation. God's got you if only you let him be God. The biggest and best revenge is no revenge. Allow God to heal your heart so you can move on, knowing that God is taking care of your problems.

Reflecting Time

Let's take some time to reflect on this issue and develop a game plan for this area of your life!

1. How has or does the enemy try to use the chains of unforgiveness to try to enslave you?

____

____

____

____

____

2. Who or what hurt you, and how?

____

____

____

____

____

3. Has forgiving them been hard? If yes, why?

____

____

____

____

____

4. How have the chains of unforgiveness tried to ruin your life?

____

____

____

____

____

5. What's holding you back from forgiving them and trusting God concerning this area of your life?

____

____

____

____

____

6. List the disadvantages of worrying.

____

____

____

____

____

7. List three ways you can start trusting God more.

____

____

____

____

____

8. List three ways you can start dismantling the chains of unforgiveness.

____

____

____

____

____

9. Are you willing to say yes to God and stop worrying?

____

____

____

____

____

10. What are you believing God for concerning this area of your life?

____

____

____

____

____

____

My Pledge

Today, I pledge to myself to never allow unforgiveness and revenge to enslave me again. I will do my best to hear from God concerning different issues that may offend me and cause me to not forgive others. Once I get directions from God, I will either let it go without explanation as I trust that God is working all things together for my good, or I will have the tough conversations led by faith and by God in order to establish an understanding for reconciliation. I will be quick to listen, slow to speak, and slow to get angry. I pledge to dismantle the chains of unforgiveness over my life through trusting God's word and working by faith, even if I do not understand it all right now.

Signature: ____

Prayer Time

Thank you, Lord, for your forgiveness! While we were yet sinners, you forgave us and died for us. You commanded your love toward us. God, give us the strength to be kind and compassionate to one another, forgiving each other just as Christ forgave us. Help us to understand the healing power of forgiveness and how impactful it is for our families and friendships! Help us to see the tricks of the enemy as he tries to tie us up in chains of unforgiveness for years. Give us the power to dismantle those chains as we walk in our freedom from offense and unforgiveness! Thank you for the victory over unforgiveness in my life.

In Jesus' name, I pray. Amen!

CHAPTER 4

Freedom from Mediocrity

Lazy hands make for poverty, but diligent hands bring wealth.

—Proverbs 10:4

God Is Calling You Higher

Your complacency keeps them comfortable. Your stagnation keeps them satisfied. Your bad breaks keep them thinking that they are better than you! People are exploiting your weaknesses. People are capitalizing off your mediocrity! They want you to stay broke, busted, and disgusted so they can take advantage of you. They don't want you to grow up because they think you will outgrow them! They want you to be mediocre your entire life. Will you live up to their standards, or will you rise up to the higher calling that God has put in your heart and mind?

The pull that you feel right now is your spirit saying it is time to stand up and fulfill your purpose by breaking the chains of mediocrity off your life. If you are tired of the same rat race that seems to get you nowhere, it's time for a change. If you are sick of the conditions that you are currently facing mentally, physically, spiritually, or financially, your time has come. If you are tired of settling for good when God has great for you, get ready! If you are tired of depending on others for security and you want to be able to take care of yourself

31

and your family, today is your day to start dismantling the chains of mediocrity on your life!

Mediocrity is a mindset or character traits that will rob you of God's best for your life. It can lead to a lifestyle of complacency and laziness. Complacency and laziness are the silent killers of your purpose and dreams. These two characteristics will trap you and lock you into a life of poverty and lack. Poverty and lack will put you in compromising situations that will make you question your morality. These situations can be as extreme as a man robbing someone to keep the heat on in the winter or a woman selling her body to put food on the table for her family. These things are not taboo; they happen all the time when you succumb to a lifestyle of mediocrity.

When you live beneath your purpose, you will settle for anything. We will work a job for forty years building someone else's dream and never try to build your own dream, even though God called us off that job after working there for five years. You learned what you needed to know. Now, it is time to invest that knowledge and effort into your dreams. Many people believe that their dreams are so farfetched that they won't even give themselves a chance to live out their dream. They allow fear to stop them. Don't let fear stop you. Build up your dream, work it with diligence, and watch how God blesses it for you.

Believe in Yourself

Do you have a dream or a vision? Have you started working toward it, or do you keep doubting yourself? What made you give up your dream? Why did you settle? Why did you stop? God gave you that dream, that idea, and that talent because he trusted you with it. Why are you doubting yourself? If God believed in you enough to give it to you, why don't you believe in yourself to do it? You can do all things through Christ Jesus who strengthens you!

You can be anything you put your mind to. You just have to try! Try it scared. Try it nervously until you get past the nervousness and start to build your confidence! It is easy to just give up, but doing it requires faith and work! What if the idea that God gave you was a multimillion-dollar idea that you are afraid to try? What if your idea is exactly what someone has been waiting for or desperately needs? People are waiting for you to get into your purpose because your purpose is connected to them as they go through life.

You Learn More from Your Failures

What is holding you back from pursuing your destiny? I believe a lot of people are afraid that they will fail. We will be so much better once we start understanding that failure is a part of the learning process. We gain so much valuable knowledge and understanding when we fail. Knowing what not to do is just as important as knowing what to do. Don't be afraid to fail or fall down; it's a part of the process. Be encouraged; no one is great at something that they just started. It takes time and practice, and you will learn as you go. You will only get better if you keep the faith and don't stop.

Fear Has to Bow Down

There are two things that can happen in your life. Either your fear is going to bow down to your faith, and you walk out of the chains of mediocrity, or your faith is going to bow down to your fear, and you will stay enslaved in chains. One is going to win. The choice is yours. I want to remind you that God will never ask you to do something that you are not equipped to do. He won't put more on you than you can bear. Nevertheless, whatever you have been given, you will be responsible and accountable for. To whom much is given, much is required.

Let's take a look at the servants that were given talents in the Bible from Matthew 25:14–30. There was one master and three servants. The master gave the first servant five talents. He gave the second servant two talents. He gave the third servant one talent. The servant with five talents made five additional talents. The servant with two talents made two additional talents. These two servants reported their profits to their master. The master told them, "Well done, good and faithful servants, you have been faithful over a little; I will set you over much."

The servant with the one talent came forward saying, "Master, I knew you to be a hard man, reaping where you did not sow, and gathering where you scattered no seed, so I was afraid, and I went and hid your talent in the ground."

The master said, "You know I reap where I have not sown, then you should have invested my money in the bank so it could have at least gained interest." The master took the talent from him and gave it to the servant that had ten talents. They say if you don't use it, you will lose it, and that is exactly what happened to this servant. He lost his talent because he did not use it because of fear.

Please don't be like this servant and lose your talent because of fear. We need your unique talents and gifts in our world. Don't let fear win! You got this!

Don't Be Status Quo

How many times have you been afraid like that servant and buried your talents, hopes, and dreams? You can no longer bury your dreams! You have to take a chance and be like the first two servants. They understood that their master had invested in them, and they made sure that they had a return when the master came back. God has invested in you, just like the master invested in them. What are you doing with your talents that he gave you? The last servant was so afraid of losing the one talent that he never even tried. He was satisfied with the status quo. He was okay with not gaining and not losing any. He was fine with being mediocre and lukewarm. God don't like people being lukewarm or status quo. Revelation 3:15–16 says, "I know your works: you are neither cold nor hot. Would that you either be cold or hot! So, because you are lukewarm, neither hot nor cold, I will spit you out of my mouth." It is not in your best interest to be lukewarm, and it is not advantageous for you to be status quo either.

Elevate Your Thinking

Why do so many people settle for less than God's best for them? It starts in their minds. Proverbs 23:7 says, "As a man thinketh in his heart so is he!" Be careful what you think about yourself. Always keep a positive outlook about yourself! Be mindful of the things that you allow to cloud your thinking. The enemy will put less than images before you and have you thinking that there is no other way. There is always a better and higher way, and although it may take more time and commitment, it will be worth it in the end. It will look like and feel like you are losing by choosing a different way and not doing it the way that most people are doing it, but believe me, you are not. I promise the grass is not greener on the other side. Most of the time, the things that you are comparing your situation with are only facades! So stop comparing your situation to others and fulfill your destiny by marching to the beat of your own drum. The world needs you, your ideas, visions, and businesses.

The enemy has tricks up its sleeve and is trying to convince you that compromising who you are will lead to getting what you want. Compromising will never give you your desired results. It will lead to headaches, heartaches, and more disappointments than you could have ever imagined. He will put images in front of you that show you only being a "side chick." The enemy is trying to convince you that the only way that you can be loved is if you settle for someone that is already committed to someone else. The devil is a liar! Let's go a little farther. The enemy has put the image of quick fame and fortune in front of you, trying to convince you that nothing is off-limits when it comes to obtaining a certain level of success, even if it requires you to compromise who you are to gain notoriety. None of these images are healthy for you, and they are designed to enslave you to this get-rich-quick mentality and mediocre mindset to keep you enslaved forever.

There are no long-lasting shortcuts that lead to desired results. You have to start casting down images and thoughts that come up in your mind that are contrary to what God says you are. You then have to step up and be the woman or man that God has called you to be. Start seeing yourself as God sees you. Stop downplaying the greatness that God has invested in you. When you downplay it, others will downplay it too. If you don't value and respect yourself, others will not value and respect you. Stop settling! Your future and legacy is contingent upon your decision to settle or rise up to the call of God for your life!

When you decide to finally choose yourself, first, and elevate your way of thinking, and you will begin to see the chains of mediocrity fall off your life. You will be awaken to a new person with a renewed sense of purpose. Sometimes, the old you will try to pull you back into your old ways, and you have to be strong enough to refuse to go back! Some people's comfort level with you will be disrupted when you become new, and that is fine. Leveling up your life and leaving mediocrity in the dust is an ongoing process, and you can't be lazy about it. Proverbs 10:4 says that "lazy hands make for poverty, but diligent hands bring wealth." You have to be committed and consistent about improving your life. If you are not diligent about this process, you will be sitting on the porch of poverty and mediocrity, watching your life pass you by. You have to motivate yourself to push harder, even when there is no one there to help motivate you. Changing and improving your life is not going to be easy, but it will be worth it. You have to have the tenacity of a bulldog when it comes to you rising above the remains of your former life!

One way that you can overcome mediocrity is by putting demand on your hands—equipping your hands and educating your mind with skills that are in demand or what you feel led to do. I remember when I was only an esthetician, I didn't have many clients. One day, my client said that she thought I would be a very good massage therapist. Just from that seed that she planted, I decided that I would look into it.

After finding the best school to meet my needs, I invested in myself and enrolled in massage school. It was not easy at all. It was very difficult for me. It was one of the hardest six months of my life, but it was so worth it because I passed my licensure test the first time. Now, I am a licensed massage therapist, and I have clients that come from all walks of life. The best thing is that I equipped my mind and hands with a skill that can never be taken away from me.

God blew my mind when he showed me that I never had to work for anyone else and that I could work for myself anywhere in the world with my massage skills. I am now a full-service spa, walking on two feet! Hallelujah! I offer full body services, from facials to waxing to massaging. This investment in me was not cheap. I am still working to pay back my student loans from this investment in myself. Breaking the chains of mediocrity will not be cheap. It will require some investment of either your time, talent, or treasure. Don't rush this process; dismantling generational chains and mindsets of mediocrity will take perseverance and determination. Be patient with yourself! Be kind to yourself. Love yourself through each phase that this process takes you!

Are you feeling a tug in your spirit to something higher or something better for you and your family? That is God gently trying to get your attention. He has his best in mind for you. He will pull greatness out of you that you didn't know was inside of you! He will tug at your spirit, but because he is a gentleman, he will not force you to do it. The trajectory of your destiny is in your hands.

God clearly spoke to me about writing this book. He also confirmed it with two men of God. I have never written a book before now, but you are currently reading my first book! The choice was mine! I had to decide to step up to the plate and answer the call or not step up and lay down in disobedience. I did it in obedience, trusting him, and I just believe that God is going to use it for my good to bless others for his glory! Amen! God told Noah to build an ark. Noah had never built an ark, but he built it because God told him to, and it saved him and his family. What has God told you to do that could save your family or even a generation? It doesn't matter if you obey or disobey; the rain is still coming!

You are where you are due to the decisions that you have made or didn't make. Please don't be dismayed because you also have the power inside of you to break the chains of mediocrity off your life and change the trajectory of your destiny. The choice is yours! You got this!

Reflecting Time

Let's take some time to reflect on this issue and develop a game plan for this area of your life!

1. How has or does the enemy try to use the chains of mediocrity to try to enslave you?

____

____

____

____

____

____

2. What caused you to stop pursuing your dream?

____

____

____

____

____

____

3. What did you settle for, and why?

____

____

____

____

____

____

4. How have the chains of mediocrity tried to ruin your life?

____

____

____

____

____

____

5. What's holding you back from God's best and keeping you at status quo?

____

____

____

____

____

6. List the advantages of pursing God's best for your life.

____

____

____

____

____

7. List three ways you can start working toward your goals.

____

____

____

____

____

8. List three ways you can start dismantling the chains of mediocrity.

____

____

____

____

____

9. Are you willing to say yes to God and start investing in yourself so you can get out of mediocrity?

____

____

____

---

10. What are you believing God for concerning this area of your life?

My Pledge

Today, I pledge to myself to never allow the chains of mediocrity to enslave me again. I will not burry my talents or the greatness that God has invested in me. I will no longer allow low-quality images to cloud my thinking with fear. I will rise above my fear and invest in myself to improve my life and legacy. I will no longer allow laziness and mediocrity to destroy my life. I will equip my mind and my hands to do the work that is required to rise above the remains of my former life. I pledge to dismantle the chains of mediocrity over my life through my faith in God and my work into myself.

Signature: ____

Prayer Time

Father, thank you for revealing this area of entrapment in my life. Thank you, Lord, that I am no longer a slave to mediocrity, complacency, and laziness. God, I pray for strength to rise above the images that are created by the enemy to destroy the greatness that you have invested in me.

No longer will I sleep on the gifts and talents that you have given me. No longer will I abandon myself and choose others over me. God, I thank you in advance for the resources needed to equip my mind and hands as I start evicting my family and myself from the low places that you have called us out of!

When the elevation process gets hard and the enemy tries to whisper, "You will never make it out of here" in my ear, be my peace, and remind me that no weapon formed against me shall prosper. Be my shield, and give me the faith to walk pass naysayers when they start saying, "You think you are better than everybody else."

Finally, help me to stop settling, and be my motivation to learn how to navigate these uncharted waters of freedom from lack to abundance, from not enough to more than enough, and from slavery to freedom. Thank you for the victory over mediocrity in my life.

In Jesus' name, I pray. Amen!

CHAPTER 5

Freedom to Be You

I praise you because I am fearfully and wonderfully made;
your works are wonderful

—Psalm 139:14

Ladies and gentlemen, I introduce to some and present to others…you! The authentic you! Nobody but you! Let me start off by reminding you that the real you is so beautiful inside and out. You have so much value. You are loved and appreciated. You are smart and successful. You are important to this world and your community. You are gifted and talented! You are blessed and highly favored! You are chosen to be exactly who and what God designed you to be. It doesn't matter what you think or feel; God has given you all that you need when he fearfully and wonderfully made you in his image. Hallelujah! I just got excited because I know that once you realize and start operating in these truths, you will be absolutely unstoppable! Glory to God!

Being the real you is one of the most powerful and liberating things that you can do in a world full of fakes and frauds. It is very rare that you meet someone that can really be themselves proudly and confidently. The question is, Why are so many people not being themselves? Do people believe that who they are is not enough? Well, if no one has told you, please know that you are enough. God made you in his image, so take a deep breath and relax. He put everything that you need inside of you. Don't ever let people say otherwise to you. Hold your head up, no matter what the enemy tries to throw at you! Don't buckle under the world's pressure to be something that you are not.

Embracing Yourself

It took me a long time to embrace myself as a kid. I was always the tallest and biggest girl in my class. I wore glasses, and I had buckteeth, with lots of gaps. I was often compared to my beautiful sisters. The only time I wasn't really in their shadows was when I played basketball. That was my safe space. I thrived in this space, and I started building my confidence in this area. Church and basketball helped me to build my authentic identity. I was the Sunday school teacher and started preaching and teaching at the age of sixteen. I remember when I finally found myself and developed a deeper relationship with God. I had torn my ACL playing college basketball, and I couldn't play anymore. I lost my identity because it was built on basketball. I remember leaving Lane College and going to Arkansas State University, where nobody knew me. That is when the cocoon of Tab started falling off. I started to evolve into Terrica, the beautiful butterfly that I am now. This transition was so hard for me but so necessary for me because I had outgrown the old me. I was evolving into the new me, and I had to find my new self.

Finding yourself can be an interesting, ongoing journey because as you grow, you will continue to evolve. Growing and evolving is a very fragile space. Take your time, and be kind to yourself in this space. While in this space, the enemy will try to plant seeds in your mind that you are less than, and that is a lie. He wants you to think that it's not cool for you to be you. Being true to yourself and saying no to things that are not good for you can make you feel isolated and alone. Be encouraged; you are not alone!

You will be faced with pressure to fit in, so you can get people to like you or make friends. Whatever you do, don't buckle under the pressure. Be true to thine own self. Stay focused on your growth and on building the right relationships. Don't lose too much sleep about the wrong relationships that didn't work or didn't fit into your world comfortably. There will be other opportunities that will serve you better.

Peer Pressure

Falling into the chains of peer pressure will enslave you because once you say yes to even the smallest things, it will lead you to saying yes to bigger and bigger things. If you let this get out of hand, it will lead you down a path of destruction. You saying no to the wrong things will eventually create opportunities for the right things to come your way. Saying no leaves space in your atmosphere for the right things to find you!

There will be peer pressure to get you to conform to the world's way. Don't bow down to it because it is not worth it! Peer pressure is like a bottomless pit that will try to consume your very life. It will have you doing and being something that you are not. It will keep you longer than you even wanted to stay. Finding the strength to say no to your peers will require courage and bravery, and that is what the three Hebrew boys demonstrated. If they can do it, you can too.

The ultimate story of overcoming peer pressure and winning in the end belongs to the three Hebrew boys. They are the prime example of facing peer pressure and standing strong. They were men of faith, and they refused to bow down to the golden idol. They had to choose between bowing to the idol or standing up for God (Daniel 3:13–30). They were brought before the king, and they told the king, "Our God whom we serve is able to deliver us from your hand, but if he doesn't, let it be known to you that we do not serve your gods, nor will we worship the gold image which you have set up" (Daniel 3:17–18). They stared down the face of peer pressure and said, "We serve the one and only true God, and we are not going to bow down to your idols."

They were thrown in a fiery furnace to be burned to death for their rebellion. The king heated the furnace seven times more than it was usually heated. They threw the boys in the furnace. The king looked inside the furnace and said, "Did we not cast three men in the midst of the fire?" He looked again and said, "I see four men loose walking in the fire that are not hurt, and the fourth man looks like the Son of God." The three Hebrew boys came out, not even smelling like smoke. The fire didn't do anything to them. The king said, "Blessed be the God of these three men." The king made a decree that any people or nation that speaks anything against their God shall be cut in pieces and their houses shall be burned to ashes because there is no other God who can deliver like this. Then the king promoted the three boys.

Not only did they refuse to bow down, but they also told the king to his face that their God would deliver them. They walked out of the seven times hotter furnace smoke-free, with no burns and with a promotion and protection that they never had before. These things were their reward for standing up for righteousness and being true to themselves. That is the type of God we serve! The world needs more courageous people like these young boys, who were not afraid to say no to what was not good for them. The world needs you to be like these young men. Someone has to stand up for what is right.

Community

The three Hebrew boys only had their belief in God and each other, and they stood up to an entire religious system and king. The bravery and faith that it took to do this is mind-blowing. Be mindful of the company you keep as it is so vital to your growth and your destiny. It is important that you find the circle that meets you where you are, but also challenges you to continue to grow to be the best you that you can be. We need others to help us navigate through the hard and low places. We also need them to help us celebrate all the amazing high places. Being there for each other through life's events is such a blessing to have as some people don't have anyone they can lean on. Be present, and reciprocate the good things. Forgive the bad things, and keep your circle strong by loving each other.

Closed Doors

You will face some type of rejection in all phases of life. We all have gone through some rejection. Rejection is inevitable; it is a part of life! Even though it is a part of life, rejection never feels good, and if I am honest, it actually hurts. So if it is a part of life and it hurts, we have to change how we see and deal with it because it is not going anywhere. We have to develop effective strategies to overcome it. When you get to a place where you value your time, energy, and effort, you will not want to waste time on things that are not for you. Please understand that every no is not designed to hurt you; most of those nos are there to direct you. I used to cry over closed doors until I saw how one closed door changed my life forever.

I had just graduated from college, and I applied for a job in my hometown. I did not get the job. I cried and cried about it. My university supervisor told me, "Don't worry about that job." He said, "I have two friends at two universities that I want you to consider going to. I am about to retire, and I want you to go to one of these schools, get your master's, and come back to take my spot here at the university." I was blown away that he thought so highly of me. I told him that I would go to the one that was closest to home. I packed up my life and moved to Tennessee.

I stayed in the Nashville area for fourteen years. It was the best thing that could have ever happened to me. I learned so much. I accomplished so much. I became a professional. I brought my first home. I started my first business. The wealth of knowledge and divine relationships that I built during that time is priceless. All of this was because someone told me no.

After looking at the benefits that came out of that no, I had to change my perspective on closed doors. I no longer feel like rejection is happening to me because I know that it is happening *for* me. Hallelujah! I just feel like praising him right now for the closed doors because I know that when the right door opens for me, God is going to give me double for my trouble! I dare you to put this book down right now and begin to praise God for the closed doors in your life! Just know that rejection comes before greatness. They rejected Jesus's parents and told them that there was no room in the inn for them right before she gave birth to greatness, and his name is Jesus. So don't you worry your pretty little head off about someone telling you no. God has something greater later in store for you!

Perfection

Remember that no one is perfect; we are all unique. Run away from people who will not allow you to be you and who demand perfection. It will take some time and intentionality to develop, mature, and perfect who you are. Allow yourself room for error and improvement. Perfection is not the key, but willingness to improve and grow is essential to the matriculation of life. Embrace and practice your uniqueness. Find your confidence through God. Once you have your confidence, please remember to always remain humble and kind.

Celebrate You

As you are growing, don't get so caught up in the imperfections and mistakes. Learn to celebrate all of your accomplishments and your growth. Take yourself out, take yourself on a vacation, go dancing, and celebrate life! Last but not least, learn to celebrate the things that make you you, like your funny personality, your body, your love for comic books, your great communication skills, your service and commitment to charity, etc. You deserve it because you have been working hard being you and loving the skin that you are in!

Be You

There is no one on this earth that is like you. You have your very own DNA, and no one can copy it. We need all your attributes and contributions! Our world would be so boring if everybody looked like each other, talked like each other, and acted like each other. God made us all unique, and it is important that we embrace our uniqueness. Never forget that you are fearfully and wonderfully made by God. You are his masterpiece!

Reflecting Time

Let's take some time to reflect on this issue and develop a game plan for this area of your life!

1. How has or does the enemy try to use the chains of peer pressure to try to enslave you?

____

____

____

____

____

____

2. Who caused you to stop being your authentic self?

____

____

____

____

____

3. What type of pressure did they apply to cause you to switch up?

____

____

____

____

____

4. How have the chains of peer pressure tried to ruin your life?

____

____

____

____

____

5. What's holding you back from being you and causing you to compromise who you are?

____

____

____

____

____

6. List and compare the advantages of trusting God and not bowing down to life's pressures.

____

____

____

____

____

7. List three ways you can start standing up to the peer pressures that you face.

____

____

____

____

____

8. List three ways you can start dismantling the chains of peer pressure.

____

____

____

____

____

9. Are you willing to trust God and be strong when you face peer pressure?

____

____

____

____

10. What are you believing God for concerning this area of your life?

____

____

____

____

____

____

My Pledge

Today, I pledge to myself to never allow peer pressure to enslave me again. When I get lost in who I am, I will go to the creator and draw near to him because he is the one who fearfully and wonderfully made me. When my old identity is trying to get the best of me, I will remember that I am no longer that person, and will rise above my old way of thinking. When I face heavy pressure, I will do my best to stand still with courage and bravery like the Hebrew boys. As I continue to grow and evolve, I will remove myself from places that no longer serve me. I will commit to putting myself in places that meet me where I am, but also challenge me to grow into a better version of myself. I pledge to dismantle the chains of peer pressure over my life through trusting God's word and working by faith.

Signature: _______________________________________

Prayer Time

Father, thank you for revealing this area of entrapment in my life. Thank you, Lord, that I am no longer a slave to peer pressure because I know who I am and whose I am. God, I pray for strength to be brave to rise above the pressures that will try to destroy my name, reputation, and my legacy.

No longer will I bow down to things that are less than the greatness that you have invested in me. God, guide me and help me to continue to shed the cocoon of the old me as I continue to evolve. Help me to spread my wings and fly to the higher places that you have called me to.

God, I thank you in advance for the divine community that will keep me accountable so I can thrive.

When it gets hard and the enemy tries to whisper, "You can't do the right thing every time," be my strength, and remind me that no weapon formed against me shall prosper. Help me to speak life into my situation when I feel hopeless.

Finally, Lord, I just want to thank you for the open doors and opportunities that you will bring before me as a reward for me saying no to the wrong things and my faithfulness to being a better me. Thank you for the victory over peer pressure in my life.

In Jesus' name, I pray. Amen!

CHAPTER 6

Freedom from Your Plans and Timeline

*"For I know the plans that I have for you," declares
the Lord, "plans to prosper you and not to harm
you, plans to give you hope and a future."*

—Jeremiah 29:11

Slow Down, and Take Your Time

Today, God whispered in my ear and said, "Tab, slow down." I had been in such a rush to meet my own deadlines that it was driving me crazy when I should have been relaxing, breathing, and taking it one day at a time. My timeline on how I wanted my life was enslaving me. Depression tried to sneak in and tell me that I was less than because I didn't have what everyone around me had. Rushing and trying to force things got me nowhere fast. After trying to force things and having things blow up in my face, it really felt more like a setback than moving forward. I would feel like I was making no progress toward my family and relationship goals. I felt like God wasn't moving on my behalf, but I would still somehow find a way to trust God, even when it seemed like there was nothing happening for me.

Living Sacrifice

As a young lady, both my parents sat me down and talked to me about dating and presenting my body as a living sacrifice. I took what they taught me to heart and began to understand that my body was the temple of the Holy Spirit. I started to understand who I was and who I belonged to. I started valuing myself more and changed my way of thinking. My standards got higher, and honestly, they put me in what felt like a hopeless situation. There had been times when I felt like no one could ever meet my standards, and this almost had me wrapped up in the chains of desperation. I truly felt like giving up. I was exhausted from all the games that people were trying to play with me. I tried dating but soon found out that it was very casual, and when you are dating with the purpose of being married, it doesn't mix well. I prayed and asked God to help me navigate this dating space because there were so many pressures that came with trying to date God's way.

I would look at other people's pictures of their family on social media, and I would feel like the grass was greener on the other side. I would feel less than for not having what they had, and I would just pray and ask God for my own family. I still pray for my family, but I get lonely and face situations that make me give up hope from time to time. Hope deferred makes the heart sick (Proverbs 13:12).

When I lose a friend that I have gotten attached to, my heart aches. While I am having my pity party, the voice from heaven reminds me that God is not slack concerning his promise toward me (2 Peter 3:9). He sees, and he knows all our needs! When we start understanding that he only has his best in mind for all of us, we will begin to trust him more when things don't work out the way we thought they should.

My Plans

I have always been an independent woman. I have always had goals and had been very ambitious. As I started getting older, I started feeling like I was watching my life pass me by. As I saw my sisters, friends, and colleagues getting married and started building their families, I would feel sad for not starting my own family. As I started getting older, and I started wondering if my biological clock would even work for me because I always wanted to have a family with three kids.

While praying for a family, I started having issues with fibroids. After the second surgery to remove the fibroids, the doctor noted that I could not carry my future children to full term because the wall of my uterus had been compromised with the two surgeries. This brought me to my knees. I felt helpless because there was nothing that I could do about it. The fibroids came back the third time, and I decided to have a partial hysterectomy to prevent them from coming back again.

After all the surgeries, I felt so defeated. I felt like I missed out on my opportunity to carry and have my own children. I felt that I would not have a legacy and that I would die alone. These dark thoughts tried to trap me in chains of heavy depression. I started feeling like there were no options or answers to my deepest desires. I was trapped in my own depression. The chains of depression weighed me down so badly until I realized that my plans for my life might not had been the plans that God had for me. I had to change my way of thinking. I had to remember that God's thoughts are not my thoughts, his ways are not my ways, and his plans are to prosper me and not harm me.

Settling Got Me Nowhere

Instead of waiting on God and preparing myself by working on the things that God told me to do, I would get bored and find myself getting involved with someone who liked me or was attracted to me. Although there were red flags, I would still try to fit him in my life. I was somewhat reckless with my heart. I would do this because I didn't want to do life alone. Life gets hard especially when you are not with your support system and family. I was living in Nashville by myself for a long time, and with all honesty, I just wanted a relationship, hoping that it would lead to love, marriage, and a family. It didn't matter that they didn't meet all my standards, I just wanted to be loved. What a terrible state to be in, butI realized that it could have been worse, so I just thank God for keeping me during those years! I finally started understanding that settling was just for the moment, and eventually, the very things that I would overlook would be the things that would cause us to break up.

Rejection Is God's Protection

After being flexible by allowing a man with red flags in my life, I would still find myself alone, feeling rejected. That feeling is a hard pill to swallow. The rejection made me feel even lonelier. It was a terrible cycle that had me bound in chains for years. I would wipe the tears from my eyes, and all I could hear was my pastor's voice in my head saying, "Terrica, rejection is God's protection." I didn't understand it, and I was just miserable doing my best to trust God through it all. The chains of this cycle were too heavy for me to bear on my own. I was enslaved by the desire to be loved prematurely by the wrong person. I was still on the potter's wheel, being shaped and molded, and I didn't even know it. It seemed like I trusted God in every area of my life, except my love life. I could believe God for houses, jobs, raises, promotion, and new cars, but not love.

Rejection is inevitable, and it is going to happen because everybody isn't for you. Everyone is not called to like or love you, so get ready! When I was rejected, I had to be careful about protecting myself by making sure that I was surrounded by my family and friends during my vulnerable moments. I also made sure that I didn't allow the enemy to get me isolated because I know that the enemy preys on the weak.

When you face rejection from others, take some time to reflect on the situation, and try to find the lesson that you had to learn. Once you learn the lesson from that situation, it is not a total loss. One of the most valuable lessons that I have ever had to learn was Proverbs 4:23: "Above all else, guard your heart, for everything you do flows from it." It's hard guarding your heart from the people that you want to see it so badly. I had to learn that I couldn't be vulnerable with everyone. I had to decrease their accessibility to me. The biggest lesson I had to learn was to not cast my pearls before swine. I could no longer waste me or my goodness on people who would not appreciate them. When people don't appreciate you, they treat you like trash, and I know that I am God's child, his masterpiece, and a queen. I had to start to being with people who understood how rare my love was and who appreciated me.

I had to learn to manage my heart by being emotionally numb because out of the heart flows everything. By doing this, it gave me the vision I needed to assess potential candidates properly. I learned that dating is just that—dating. Gathering data to determine if this person is equally yoked with you spiritually, physically, financially, mentally, and emotionally. The energy and chemistry can be amazing when you are with them, but if their values, morals, and lifestyle don't align with yours, it will not work. When it didn't work, I couldn't keep crying about it; I had to move on. Separation, breaking up, or being rejected is never easy, but I found that it doesn't have to be that hard either. When you trust God, you will realize that it wasn't your fault or their fault; it was actually God closing a door and moving what wasn't designed for you out of your way. God told me, "You didn't ruin it. I removed it. What I have coming is better!"

Once those people are out of your way, you are ready for what he has specifically for you. You also understand that he has your back and he knows what's best for you. After reflecting on the lessons learned from that situation, take some time to thank God for what didn't happen, and take that knowledge and apply it to your life when needed.

I Dodged a Bullet

When I look back at the men that I went to God about concerning my heart, my soul looks back and wonder how I got over. All I can say is thank you, God, for not giving me what I was asking you for! I look back and say, "Oh my goodness, I dodged a bullet!" Hallelujah! Sometimes, I say I dodged a drive by! I'm glad he didn't give me what I wanted because I couldn't foresee that my purpose didn't align with those young men's purposes. I am blessed that he is my father, and he knows what I need. I am truly blessed that he gave me other desires by molding my heart and my vision to see and want the things that he wants for me!

There is nothing wrong with wanting the things that God wants for you! He only wants the absolute best for you! There are times when I reflect on how he kept me, even when I couldn't keep myself. Some of you may not understand how it feels to be loved and safe in the arms of a good, good father! When I think of the goodness of God and all that he has done for me, my soul says, "Hallelujah, thank you for saving me! Thank you for saving me from that bullet."

While I Was by Myself

I have spent almost all of my adulthood living by myself and finding my own way. After experiencing some things in life and watching God move in other areas of my life, I finally got a revelation one day. I realized that although I had accomplished a lot on my own in life, I was not prepared for what I was asking God for, and there were still some things that God wanted me to do alone while he had my full attention. I didn't like this revelation at all because I felt like I had done enough on my own, and I was tired of being alone. When I got this revelation, I was like, "Really, God, what else could you want me to do by myself?" I had already got the degrees, jobs, house, car, and businesses. I couldn't think of anything else that I needed to do. My situation looked very bleak. It seemed like I had been working and preparing my entire life, and all I wanted was to finally be loved by the right person and have a family.

I will never forget I was at a church and Bishop McIntosh prophesied to me about this book. After church service, my sisters, my mom, and I started talking about how on point his prophecy was concerning me. My oldest sister asked me if I heard him when he said, "God allowed you to do this while you were by yourself. God is establishing you, your ministry, your brand, and your life while you were by yourself."

I told her, "No, I didn't remember." She told me to go back and listen to it again. She also expressed that she believed that the things that I had been praying for were contingent upon me completing this book.

I went back and listened to it, and my entire life changed from that moment. I knew from that point on that God was preparing and establishing me before he released me for greater things. I started moving differently. I started moving with more urgency because I knew that I was being prepared for his purpose. I started getting a better understanding of why my life had been, what it had been, and the chains of wanting to be loved by the right person at the wrong time started falling off me. Hallelujah! God began to free me. He freed my mind and calmed my spirit and my longing for premature love. He also reminded me that the wait was not punishment, but it was in fact a "preparation for my next level."

Your Single Season aka Sowing Season Is Vital

While I was quickly rushing in a race that I never even wanted to be in, God was slowly chipping away at my fleshly desires and molding me into the woman that I am right now. His plans for my life were way better than my plans! I am a confident woman of God, who understands that God's timing is not like our timing. I also understand that for everything, there is a season and a time for every matter under heaven (Ecclesiastes 3:1). Understanding the principle of seed time and harvest has helped me process this single season in my life. I understand that this is not just my single season, but it is in fact my sowing season as well. I know that my harvest will be great if I keep planting good seeds and if I wait on the Lord! So if you are in a single season, keep your head up during this time, and don't let your sowing season get you down! Harvest is coming soon! Always try your best to sow good seeds as much as possible because you will reap a good harvest if you do! Find things that you enjoy doing, and do them. Don't wait for anyone to enjoy your life. Invest in yourself during this time. Do what makes you happy!

It is Due Season

Please know that God has not forgotten you, and it is due season! He has plans to prosper you and not harm you. Prosperity is your portion! Success is your portion. I am super-duper excited about your harvest season! I am just as excited for you as I am for myself. It doesn't matter what you have been sowing for! Maybe your sowing season was you working for many years at a job, and you finally got that promotion or raise. I am excited for you! Maybe you finally got the house that you had been saving for, sacrificing for, dreaming for, and praying for. I am excited for you! Maybe you had been working steadfastly, trying to build your business up, and you finally got the consistent clientele that you needed to finally get your own building. I am excited for you! Maybe your sowing season was you fighting a terminal illness, and God healed and delivered you from the choke hold of death! I am excited for you!

I am excited for everyone that started with nothing but the faith of a mustard seed and hard work! I am excited because guess what? It is due season! I dare you to just throw your hands up now and start thanking God for your due season! You have sowed years and tears, and it is finally time for you to get yours! Lord, I thank you for the due seasons that are quickly approaching for each and every one of your children that are reading this book right now! God, give them double for the trouble for what they had to endure! Restore the years and what the cankerworm had eaten, and enlarge their territory. Glory to God, and hallelujah! Lord, I thank you that you are never late and you are always on time!

Reflecting Time

Let's take some time to reflect on this issue and develop a game plan for this area of your life!

1. How has or does the enemy try to use the chains of premature desires to try to enslave you?

____
____
____
____
____

2.   What premature desires do you struggle with the most?

____
____
____
____
____

3.   Are these desires causing you to settle? If yes, how have you started settling?

____
____
____
____
____

4.   How have the chains of premature desires tried to ruin your life?

____
____
____
____
____

5.   What premature desires are standing in the way of God's purpose and plans for your life?

____
____
____
____
____

6. List and compare the advantages of giving up your desires and waiting on God.

____

____

____

____

____

7. List three ways you can invest in yourself during your sowing season.

____

____

____

____

____

8. List three ways you can start dismantling the chains of premature desires.

____

____

____

____

____

9. Are you willing to accept rejection as God's direction no matter what?

____

____

____

____

____

10. What are you believing God for concerning this area of your life?

____

____

____

____

____

____

My Pledge

Today, I pledge to myself to never allow my plans or timeline to enslave me again. I will trust God at his word. I will walk in confidence, knowing that he has plans for me—plans to prosper me and not harm me. I will no longer rush or force anything with anyone. I will allow God to manifest his blessing for me. I will no longer settle by casting my pearls before swine, who do not have the capacity to even understand my value or worth. When I face rejection, I will move accordingly because I know that that's God's protection for me. I pledge to invest in myself and others during my single and sowing season. I pledge to dismantle the chains of premature desires over my life through trusting God's word and working by faith, even if I do not understand it all right now.

Signature: ____

Prayer Time

Father, thank you for revealing this area of entrapment in my life and breaking those chains off. Thank you, Lord, that I am no longer a slave to my own plans, timeline, and premature desires. Thank you that they are no longer my masters and can no longer dictate what I do and how I live.

As I navigate this single and sowing season, please help me to enjoy it more. Help me to enjoy my family and friends along the way. Teach me how to use this time alone wisely. Open my eyes and my heart to the experiences and lessons that I will encounter on my journey. Help me to gain wisdom, knowledge, and understanding from them so that I may be able to help someone else along the way. Open my eyes to the divine connections that you will arrange for me during this time. Allow me to take advantage of the opportunities that you present during this season.

Give me the motivation to take full advantage of my sowing season. As I begin building a better life for myself, please give me the strength and wisdom to invest in every area of my life. Continue to increase my understanding of the purpose and plans that you have for me. I know that you only have what's best for me, but sometimes, my vision gets blurry with tears. When I can't trace you working behind the scenes for me, please help me to trust you more.

Empower me with the strength to resist the urge to settle for less than the standards. Hold my hand and my heart steady so I will not buckle under the pressure to cast my pearls before swine. I ask that you guide me along the way, especially when I get lonely. Help me to guard my heart with people who don't have my best interest at heart. Please always send me gentle reminders that you will never leave or forsake me and that you have not forgotten about me.

God, I trust your timing, and when you see fit for me to have the love and family that you have specifically designed for me, no one will be able to take the credit for it, and no one will be able to take it from me. Thank you for my journey because I know that there is purpose behind it all because you are a purposeful God! Thank you for the victory over my premature desires and plans in my life.

In Jesus' name, amen.

CHAPTER 7

Freedom from Ignorance and Destruction

My people are destroyed for the lack of knowledge.

—Hosea 4:6

Knowledge Is Power

Wake up, and gird up your lions! We are in a spiritual warfare every single day! Although the enemy comes to kill, steal, and destroy, oftentimes, it's not even the enemy that is destroying us. We are destroying ourselves due to our very own ignorance. No longer can we take the education process lightly. Our lives are dependent upon it!

Ignorance equals self-destruction! Ignorance is the lack of knowledge or information. Ignorance is a weed that will grow up and choke the very life out of you! Once you cease learning, you stop growing, but the weeds of ignorance will continue to grow up like a forest that will consume you. There are people who have systematically tried to oppress you because of your ignorance. Ignorance is dangerous!

Knowledge equals power! Knowledge is the skills acquired by a person through education, experience, or exposure. Power is the ability to direct or influence others. Knowledge and power are good, but wisdom is better than both of them. Wisdom is when you know how and when to use knowledge and power for the greater good.

Wisdom is knowledge applied to your situation at the right time and the right place. Knowledge and wisdom are the secret weapons we have in order to win this spiritual war and to escape the chains of destruction. If we don't acquire these, we are doomed to living a disenfranchised and unfulfilled life, filled with struggles and destruction. The lack of knowledge perpetuates cycles of poverty, destruction of individuals, families, communities, and society as a whole. Knowledge is the key to dismantling the chains of ignorance.

Comfortability in Ignorance

The chains of ignorance have enslaved and destroyed people for generations. We are living in one of the most informative eras in history, and ignorance is still running rampant and decapacitating people left and right. Dr. Martin Luther King Jr. once said, "Nothing is more dangerous than sincere ignorance and conscientious stupidity." The phrase that stuck out to me the most from his quote was "sincere ignorance." That means they are wholeheartedly committed to being ignorant and lazy because they are comfortable not knowing. They are also not willing to do the work to get an understanding of things. They honestly prefer to stay ignorant. They have a long-standing love affair with ignorance because there is no accountability when you don't know. Ignorance puts you at a constant disadvantage and can lead to a very difficult life. That life can leave you at the mercy of others while feeling defenseless, helpless, incapable, and vulnerable. Ignorance will cause people to just say yes to anything. Saying yes to everything will entrap you to others and leave you at their mercy, stuck in what they want you to do as their slave.

Being Assertive and Intentional about Your Life

You cannot be lazy when it comes to your life or learning. Nobody is obligated to do anything for you after you turn eighteen.

There are no handouts in life. Your destiny lies in your own hands. Your life will be what you make of it. If you don't build it the way that you want it to be, life will come in and demolish any hope that you could have ever had for your future. We live in a cold, cold world, and if you are not assertive and intentional about your life, you will find yourself in very low and tight spaces. Those tight spaces will have your back up against the wall, facing circumstances that will drag you from rut to rut and keep you in a rat race as long as possible!

I remember a time when I felt like life was dragging me like a dog. I would fight traffic for an hour to get to work. When I got to work, I would fight students to stay in class. I would fight teachers to keep their students in class. I was breaking up riots and fights. I would fight traffic for an hour and fifteen minutes going home. I felt like I was at war with my life. That job was robbing me of my peace every day. I was overworked and underpaid. I was mentally and physically exhausted every day! These are stressors that no one should put themselves under. If you are experiencing these stressors, I want to encourage you to remove yourself from that situation and protect your peace.

One day, it finally hit me like a ton of bricks. I had a feeling of discontent that took over my entire body. I was not satisfied with where I was, and it took me a while to understand that I had outgrown that place. I also realized that what I had built was no longer serving me. Have you ever worked hard for a degree, job, promotion, friendship, or relationship, and it just didn't turn out the way you thought that it would? How devastating it is to see it all fall apart! That is exactly how I felt, and I was so stressed out because it didn't work for me! I was experiencing growing pains. God was shifting me, and he was giving me new desires. There will be times in life when you grow out of old spaces, places, and faces. You will feel pulled toward new things. Your vision and desires will change. You will finally decide that you deserve better, and you will not let anyone stop you. God is a progressive God, and he will do a new thing in your life if only you would let him. The change that you are seeking is inside of your faith in the new vision that you have for yourself and your family. Where God gives vision, he also gives provision to accomplish it for your good and his glory!

The enlightening moment that woke me up was an undeniable urgency that made me take charge of my life. It was like God was speaking in Proverbs 6:6–8 to me. I could hear him saying to me, "You can do and be anything you want to be if you are willing to do the work." He reassured me that he would take my natural efforts and add his super to it to create a supernatural blessing for me. Some people don't want to put forth the natural efforts needed to create a supernatural blessing. God can do anything but fail, but he is a gentleman, and he will not force his will upon your life. He needs to know that you are ready for his supernatural blessings through your natural efforts!

Once I began to understand what God was saying to me, I began changing my life by faith and lots of hard work! I became more assertive, and I began to drag life as I was in pursuit of a better life for myself. I had to be intentional about the decisions that I was making because your decisions take you to your destination and your future. Starting over was very hard, and I am not going to pretend like it wasn't. Nevertheless, my determination would not let me stop! Once I got my momentum going, it was like riding a bike. I resigned from my administration job and went back to school to pursue my entrepreneurial dream of being a spa owner and as an esthetician. What do you need to be determined about? What decisions do you have to be intentional about to ensure a better future for you?

Empowered Through 3 Es

Knowledge is a wellspring that never stops flowing, and it is vital to your continual growth and freedom. If there is no learning or knowledge, you will be destroyed. That's why we are warned in 1 Peter 5:8 to be sober minded and alert because our enemy is prowling, trying to take us out any way that he possibly can. We become alert and sober minded through education, experience, and exposure. After we have experienced and embraced these things, we will be empowered to execute the challenges we face with the spirit of excellence. We will be able to fight the good fight. We will be able to tackle the disparities that put us at a disadvantage and try to keep us on unequal playing fields.

Education. Starting over and going back to college is never easy. Even as an educator and administrator of fourteen years, it was still challenging. Nevertheless, I committed to the process of education to change my life because I was miserable with what I was doing. This was one of the toughest seven months of my life. I was not working, and I was living off my retirement from my previous job. There was no money coming in, and money was flying away left and right. I understood that the sacrifice that I was making would eventually pay off for me.

The schoolwork was a breeze for me, but the school environment was hostile, and the condition of the school was not ideal. I had to learn to keep my thoughts to myself and overcome the adversities as they presented themselves. I refused to quit because failure was not an option for me. I was banking on myself, and no one had my back but me! No one was going to do it for me. I had to be assertive and intentional about it because I couldn't let myself down. I had too much depending on me!

When you are doing something good or positive for yourself, there will be some haters that come your way. Don't let them distract you! Stay on the wall, and complete the work that is in front of you. While on my journey, I had some people who didn't believe in me or my dream, and that was fine because God didn't give them my vision. However, there was this one particular naysayer that thought I was dumb just because of where I was from. I met him at a comedy show, and he asked me where I was from. I told him, and he looked at me and said, "Can you read?" I was livid, but that is what he really thought about me and my city. I was in disbelief, honestly! I quickly answered that question and let him know about my extensive educational background. He looked at me and could not believe that I was from there.

I was so glad that I was able to set the record straight concerning me and my city. This encounter just reminded me that there are some people who will not believe in you and think that you are dumb just because of where you are from. There are some naysayers that will come just to plant seeds of negative words and thoughts, but you cannot let them stop or block your growth and development. Imagine if I wasn't confident in who I am and whose I am, I would have probably been discouraged and would have given up, but I didn't because I believe in myself and God. There is nothing anyone can say to stop me. Always believe in yourself and have confidence in who you are and who you are becoming every day. It doesn't matter what room you step into. You were invited because someone saw something in you. When you get there, smile, and listen more than you speak. When it's time to speak, ask God to give you the words to say!

I never stopped or gave up on my pursuit to improve my life. The rewards of accomplishing my goal improved my life and afforded me the lifestyle that I desired and worked hard for. I took the time to equip my mind and my hands to be skilled enough to provide a very nice life for myself. It was not easy, but it was worth it. I also know that no one can ever take my education from me. It is mine and mine alone! No one can take your education from you either. Once you got it, it's yours!

Your education, be it a degree or skill set, will be what you make of it. Your education is personal, and no one can do it for you. It is your very own personal development. The skills that you acquire will be contingent upon how you pursue them. You have to have the tenacity of a bulldog to overcome any and all obstacles that try to come between you and your dreams. I come from a place where there aren't many options, and if that is what you are facing, don't let that stop you. Go forth and follow your dreams, even if it takes you away from home for a season. Don't stop until you are satisfied and you have dismantled the chains of ignorance and destruction over your life.

Exposure and Experience. Anything that you do that is positive or for the betterment of your life will be challenging. Don't run from or pray away every obstacle that you face in pursuit of your education and future. That exposure to that obstacle is teaching and giving you the experience that you will need in life at some point. It is also teaching you how to trust God more in the face of adversity.

Paul was given a thorn in his flesh, and he sought the Lord three times about the thorn in his flesh. Just like Paul had to go through this exposure to this thorn in his flesh, God will expose you to difficulty to develop you and teach you experiences that you need for future challenges. The development will be intense, but the reward and experience will be priceless! Oftentimes, experience is the best teacher.

You will learn more from your failures than from your success. Don't let it stop you. Failure builds character that will be needed to keep you in the places that your education will take you. Don't let the challenge steal your victory. Remember that God will not put more on you than you can bear. His grace is sufficient for you!

I remember when I was first learning how to do balloon decor. My goodness, what a journey that was. It was a rough learning curve for me, but I eventually got it. I was first introduced to it by a colleague of mine. She showed me a picture of two Mickey Mouse balloon columns. I didn't think anything of it until one of my friends came to my birthday party and told me that he really liked how I had decorated, and he wanted me to decorate for his birthday party. Immediately, I remembered the picture that she showed me, and I went to her and asked her if she could show me how to do it. She told me that all I needed was on YouTube. I started watching all the videos that I could learn from. I eventually learned all I could from those videos. I signed up to go to a balloon conference and surrounded myself with the balloon experts. I learned so much from those people that I started doing balloons for others. People started seeing my work, and they kept calling. I got so busy with it that I opened my balloon decor business and got my LLC. I have been doing balloons for almost ten years, and I have enjoyed it.

It just blows my mind that I got started in this industry because she showed me that one picture. Now, she contacts me and asks me to show her new techniques from time to time. She exposed me to it, and I took the time to learn the skill with the tenacity of a bulldog.

Now, those balloons pay some of my bills and serve as another stream of income for me. I thank God for the simple exposure—and now the experience—that continues to open doors for me! Amen. Don't be opposed to trying and experiencing new things. You never know what God has in store for you from the exposure.

In All Thy Getting, Get Understanding/Wisdom

Once you have acquired knowledge and wisdom through education, exposure, and experience, doors will open for you, and opportunities will come. When you get to these places, take your time getting to know the people that you will be assigned to serve. Getting an understanding of your people is vital to your success because people don't care what you know until they know that you care. When you develop your understanding and care for your people, start applying the knowledge and wisdom to develop your leaders and build your teams! After you have completed this, nothing shall be impossible for you all.

A true understanding with your people and your team will make you all unstoppable. Genesis 11:1–7 explains how the people were on one accord with their communication and understanding that they were able to build a tower so high that it reached the heavens, and it got God's attention. God came down to see the city and the tower the people were building. He looked at it and said, "If as one people speaking the same language, they have begun to do this, then nothing they plan to do will be impossible for them. Come, let us go down and confuse their language so they will not understand each other." When you have great knowledge, wisdom, and understanding, nothing can stop you as an individual or as a team. You can do the impossible, just like they did in the Bible.

As an educator, I am an advocate for education and learning because I know that where there is no knowledge, there is darkness. I also know where there is darkness, there is void, emptiness, lack, and an enemy waiting there to ambush. As long as you are in the dark or are ignorant, you have the potential to be manipulated, exploited, abused, and trapped. He is coming to kill, steal, and destroy through the chains of ignorance and destruction.

God Will Be There for You

I want to encourage you to get in spaces that are conducive for learning. Get around others that are smarter than you, and just listen. You will gain a wealth of knowledge by just being around them. No matter how deep or dark the river of ignorance you are in, don't fear because God will be with you. Isaiah 43:2 says, "When you pass through the waters, I will be with you; and when you pass through the rivers, they will not sweep over you. When you walk through the fire, you will not be burned; the flames will not set you ablaze." He promised that he will be there for you because he loves you. Take it one day at a time with this promise in your heart that he will be with you every step of the way! Amen!

Reflecting Time

Let's take some time to reflect on this issue and develop a game plan for this area of your life!

1. How has or does the enemy try to use the chains of ignorance to try to enslave you?

____

____

____

____

____

2. What areas of life do you want to become more knowledgeable in?

____

____

____

____

---

3. How has this lack of knowledge affected you or your family?

____

____

____

____

4. How have the chains of ignorance tried to ruin your life?

____

____

____

____

5. What are the advantages of equipping yourself with knowledge?

____

____

____

____

6. What are the disadvantages of not being equipped with knowledge?

____

____

____

____

7. List three ways you can gain more education, experience, and exposure to become wiser.

____

____

____

____

____

8. List three ways you can start dismantling the chains of ignorance.

____

____

____

____

____

9. Are you willing to do the work to improve your life and your family's life?

____

____

____

____

____

10. What are you believing God for concerning this area of your life?

____

____

____

____

____

My Pledge

Today, I pledge to myself to never allow the chains of ignorance enslave me again. Once the lack of knowledge has been shown to me, I vow to do my best to become educated in that area. After I have tried my best to understand and I still can't get it, I promise to seek help from others. I will do my best to be a life-long learner and to stay abreast of the things that challenge me the most. I refuse to allow ignorance to run ramped in my life or in my family. I will be an advocate for education, experience, and exposure. No longer will I be afraid or ashamed to let people know that I do not understand. I will strive for understanding in every area of my life.

I pledge to dismantle the chains of ignorance and destruction over my life through trusting God's word and working by faith in my pursuit of knowledge and understanding.

Signature: ____

Prayer Time

Father, thank you for revealing this area of entrapment in my life and breaking the chains of ignorance and destruction off my life.

Lord, I ask that you would crown my head with wisdom, knowledge, and understanding in the areas where I lack. You said that if we ask for wisdom, you would give it liberally. Please give me the strength to be assertive and intentional concerning my life and my learning. Father, help me to be a life-long learner, and don't allow myself to be exploited, abused, or misused by scammers that are trying to take advantage of me. Expose every wolf in sheep clothing that are digging ditches, trying to trap me through my lack of knowledge.

Give me the grace to start over if I need to. Be a lamp unto my feet, and show me the way to improving my life. Order my steps through each phase of my learning process. When things get hard for me along the way, help me to lean not unto my own understanding, but in all my ways, to acknowledge you as you shall direct my path.

Let your power rest on me as I overcome the thorns and challenges that come with the learning curves that I will face. Be my pilot, and help navigate me through this learning space efficiently and expeditiously. Give me common sense and book sense to keep me balanced in this classroom that we call life.

Hold my hand, and cover my heart as you take me through the necessary life lessons and storms to produce the greatness that you have planted inside of me before I was in my mother's womb.

Help me to be more flexible and trustworthy in you since you know what's best for me and you know what I need in order to be free from ignorance and destruction. Thank you for the victory over the destruction of ignorance in my life.

In Jesus' name, I pray. Amen.

CHAPTER 8

Freedom from Fear

God has not given us the spirit of fear,
but of love and of a sound mind.

—2 Timothy 1:7

No weapon formed against me shall prosper.

—Isaiah 54:17

Fear is an emotion that we have all experienced from what we believe is a danger or a threat to us. Fear triggers the natural physiological response of fight or flight in us to protect us from harm. When we find ourselves in dangerous situations, we are either going to fight or run for our lives.

We all face many forms of fear that try to enslave us, but we have to remember that fear does not come from God because he has not given us the spirit of fear! The chains of fear from your past, present, or even future will try to entrap your mind and make you feel like you are all by yourself in this world! Fear will play on your emotions and will have you thinking that everyone is out to get you, and it will have you paranoid to the point of no return.

I deal with the fear of the unknown from time to time. As a very detailed and organized person, not knowing what's going to happen sets me off into a tailspin. I sit and overthink about all the negative possible situations that could happen. I also have a few backup plans just in case something goes wrong. Oftentimes, I talk myself out of doing things just to play it safe so I won't get hurt.

Moving from city to city triggers fear in me as a single woman. I have anxiety not knowing if I will be safe or if I will meet new people who will accept me as their own. Starting over by myself is hard, and it causes me to be afraid to even try. When I was younger, this was not an issue for me. As I have matured, I don't see the world as I did when I was young and naïve, and the world has changed a lot since then.

Don't Let Others Create Fear or Doubt in You

When you are believing God for something, there will be times when you face haters that will try to create fear in you by discouraging you. They will say things like, "You can't do that" or "Who do you think that you are?" There will be naysayers that say and do just about anything to shut you and your vision down.

Mark 10:46–52 says that Bartimaeus heard that Jesus was passing by, and he began crying out saying, "Jesus, Son of David, have mercy on me!" The haters around him warned him to be quiet, but he cried out all the more. "Son of David, have mercy on me!" Jesus stood still and commanded him to come.

After Jesus called him, the haters started saying, "Be of good cheer. Rise, He is calling you." They went from telling him to shut up to telling him to be of good cheer. People will hate you and try to discourage you. Then they will turn around and use the same mouth to cheer you on. Don't let others create fear or doubt in you. When you set your mind to do something, pray about it, and move when God says it's time for you to move. People will be jealous of you just because you have motion or vision for your life and they don't.

Bartimaeus was blind physically, but he still had vision and motion for his life. He knew what he needed, so he got up and went to Jesus. Jesus asked him what he wanted. He told Jesus, "That I may receive my sight."

Then Jesus said to him, "Go your way; your faith has made you well." And immediately, he received his sight and followed Jesus on the road. Just because God didn't give others your vision doesn't mean you stop pursuing it. He didn't stop, no matter what they said to discourage him or to cause him to be afraid. He pressed his way to Jesus while he was still blind. Hallelujah! Sometimes, you have to see past what you are seeing in the physical realm before it can manifest itself.

Blind Bartimaeus wouldn't let the haters intimidate him while he was trying to get his blessing. Stop letting the words or actions of others hold you back. Remember what Isaiah 54:17 says, "No weapon formed against me shall prosper!" It won't work! Start building yourself up with the word each day. Start declaring God's word over your life, and start moving in it! Your thoughts create your words, and your words create your world. Start speaking only positive words over your life.

Once you get God's word in your spirit and in your mouth, you combat the enemy when he tries to feed you a lie. Combat his lies with God's word, and let him know that you are the head and not the tail, first and not last, above only and never beneath, and lender to many nations and not the borrower. Let him know that you are blessed in the city and in the field, blessed when you come and when you go, the fruit of your body is blessed, the fruit of your land is blessed, and everything your hands touch prospers.

Don't Let Giants Stop You

Have you ever been so afraid of something, and when you finally face it, you realize it's not as bad as you thought it would be? Our imagination can get wild and will have our mind playing tricks on us. When we face things that appear to be bigger than us, we tend to back down to it. There will be times when you are not able to back down from it, and you will have to face it with the greater one that lives inside of you (John 4:4).

Israel was being bullied by Goliath, the giant champion. He came out and threatened them for forty days, and King Saul and the

Israelites were terrified. David was taking food to his brothers, and he heard Goliath defying Israel. David started asking about him and told King Saul that he would go against Goliath. King Saul and his own brothers didn't believe in David. He told David that he was too young, and Goliath had been a warrior since his youth. David told King Saul, "I have killed a lion and a bear, and Goliath will be like one of them. The Lord who rescued me from the lion and the bear will rescue me from this Philistine." David had seen the Lord take and keep him through those battles, and he had confidence that God would not let him fall in this battle.

They tried to dress him in their armor, but David couldn't fit them, so he took them off. He got five smooth stones from the stream. Goliath went after David with a sword, spear, and a javelin. David said, "I come against you in the name of the Lord Almighty, whom you have defied, and today, the Lord will deliver you into my hands." Goliath tried to attack David, but David pulled out a stone and his slingshot and slung the stone. It hit Goliath in the head and killed him. The young boy with just a stone and slingshot killed the enemy's biggest warrior. He didn't use anything fancy to kill him. He used a rock and killed the biggest threat that Israel had ever seen or gone against.

Life Lessons

There are so many takeaways from this amazing story of faith and bravery. I just want to emphasize a few. Number one: Don't run from those small challenges because they prepare you for the giants that you will face later. Those challenges develop your faith, strength, and confidence in yourself and God. It reminds you that nothing shall be impossible. Number two: Believe in yourself! Don't ever doubt who you are, who you are becoming, and who you belong to. Don't let people try to tell you about you. Other people's opinion of you don't matter. Know who you are! Folks will try to discourage you just because they can't do something that you can do. Number three: Believe in God! If he brought you to it, he will bring you through it. He prepared the stage for you, and all you have to do is show up and watch God show out on your behalf. He is going to take your natural, add his super to it, and create a supernatural experience just because you showed up with faith in him! If you take these approaches when you are facing physical, mental, spiritual, or financial giants, you will win! The fight is fixed, and the victory is already yours!

Psalm 91:1–16 AMP

When I am facing fear, I go to one of my favorite chapters in the Bible—Psalm 91. This chapter soothes all my fears and calms all of my anxiety by reassuring me that God is my protector and provider.

The Protection When You Are in His Presence

He who dwells in the secret place of the Most High will remain secure *and* rest in the shadow of the Almighty [whose power no enemy can withstand].
I will say of the LORD, "He is my refuge and my fortress, My God, in whom I trust [with great confidence, and on whom I rely]!"
For He will save you from the trap of the fowler,
And from the deadly pestilence.
He will cover you *and* completely protect you with His feathers, And under His wings you will find refuge;
His faithfulness is a shield and a wall. (Psalm 91:1–4 AMP)

No Matter Day or Night He is Always There for You

You will not be afraid of the terror of night,
Nor of the arrow that flies by day,
Nor of the pestilence that stalks in darkness,

Nor of the destruction (sudden death) that lays waste at noon.

A thousand may fall at your side And ten thousand at your right hand,

But danger will not come near you.

You will only observe with your eyes

And witness the punishment and repayment of the wicked. (Psalm 91:5–8 AMP)

The Protection because You Made the Lord Your Dwelling

Because you have made the LORD, [who is] my refuge, Even the Most High, your dwelling place,

No evil will befall you,

Nor will any plague come near your tent.

For He will command His angels in regard to you,

To protect *and* defend *and* guard you in all your ways [of obedience and service].

They will lift you up in their hands,

So that you do not [even] strike your foot against a stone.

You will tread upon the lion and cobra;

The young lion and the serpent you will trample underfoot. (Psalm 91:9–13 AMP)

The Protection because You Love Him

"Because he set his love on Me, therefore I will save him; I will set him [securely] on high, because he knows My name [he confidently trusts and relies on Me, knowing I will never abandon him, no, never].

"He will call upon Me, and I will answer
him; I will be with him in trouble; I will rescue
him and honor him.
"With a long life I will satisfy him
And I will let him see My salvation." (Psalm
91:14–16 AMP)

The Names of God to Call for Protection and Provision

Everything—Call on the name of Jehovah Elohim. He is the God
who is in control of everything.
Healing—Call on the name of Jehovah Rapha. He is the God who
heals.
Peace—Call on the name of Jehovah Shalom. He is the God of peace.
Provision—Call on the name of Jehovah Jireh. He is the God who
provides.

Scriptures to Stand on and Believe When You Face Fear or Adversity

Fear—Psalm 27:1—"The Lord is my light and salvation who shall I
fear, the Lord is the strength of my life of who shall I be afraid."
Attacks—Isaiah 54:17—"No weapon formed against me shall prosper!" (It won't work! Hallelujah!)
Deliverance—Psalm 18:2—"The Lord is my rock and my fortress
and my deliverer."
Strength—Philippians 4:13—"I can do all things though Christ that
strengthens me."
Overcoming—Romans 8:37—"We are more than conquerors
through Him that love us."

Reflecting Time

Let's take some time to reflect on this issue and develop a game plan for this area of your life!

1. How has or does the enemy try to use the chains of fear to try to enslave you?

____

____

____

____

____

2. What areas of life do you suffer with fear the most?

____

____

____

____

____

3. How has fear affected your past, present, and future?

____

____

____

____

____

4. How has fear affected your confidence and self-esteem?

____

____

____

____

____

5. How can you start building your confidence and self-esteem back up?

____

____

____

____

____

6. What are the disadvantages of operating in fear?

____

____

____

____

____

7. List three ways you can increase your faith in God over your fear.

____

____

____

____

____

8. List three ways you can start dismantling the chains of fear.

____

____

____

____

____

9. Are you willing to do the work to move out of fear into faith?

____

____

____

____

———————————————————

———————————————————

10. What are you believing God for concerning this area of
your life?

———————————————————

———————————————————

———————————————————

———————————————————

———————————————————

———————————————————

My Pledge

Today, I pledge to myself to never allow the chains of fear to enslave me again. No matter how great or small the image of fear may be in my sight, it will bow down to my faith. From this point on, I will see impossible situations as opportunities for God to show up and show out on my behalf. God specializes in impossible situations. Yes, though I walk through the valley of the shadow of death, I will fear no evil because God is with me, and he will never leave or forsake me. No longer will I allow my imagination to run wild concerning things that make me afraid. I will cast down my imaginations and every high thing that exalts itself against the knowledge of God, and I will bring into captivity every thought to obedience of Christ. I will always remember that the greater one lives inside of me and those who are with me are greater than those who are against me. Nothing shall be impossible for me. When I feel fear trying to come into my life, I will face it head on, with God by my side, knowing that we will win!

Signature: _______________________________________

Prayer Time

Father, thank you for revealing this area of entrapment in my life and breaking the chains of fear and anxiety off my life. Lord, I stand on your word that you shall deliver me. You have never failed, and you won't start now. Thank you for covering me and being my shield. Thank you for being my refuge.

Lord, thank you for dispatching your angels before, behind, and beside me. Thank you for giving me the strength to speak to any giant or mountain and say, "Be thou cast into the sea." Thank you, Lord, that no evil shall befall me, neither shall any plaque come near my dwelling.

No matter what the enemy is saying to me or trying to get me to believe, I will stand on your word in Psalm 27:1–3, 5–6:

> The Lord is my light and my salvation; whom shall I fear?
> The Lord is the strength of my life; of whom shall I be afraid?
> When the wicked, even my enemies and my foes came upon me to eat up my flesh they stumbled and fell.
> Though a host should encamp against me my heart shall not fear; though war should rise against me, in this will I be confident.
>
> For in the time of trouble He shall hide me in his pavilion;
> in the secret of His tabernacle shall he hide me;
> he shall set me up upon a rock.
> And now shall mine head be lifted up above mine enemies round me: therefore, will I offer in his tabernacle sacrifices of joy;
> I will sing, yea I will sing praises unto the Lord.

In Jesus' name, I pray. Amen.

CHAPTER 9

Freedom from Sin

*If you declare with your mouth, "Jesus is Lord,"
and believe in your heart that God raised him from the
dead, you will be saved. For it is with your heart
that you believe and are justified, and it is with your
mouth that you profess your faith and are saved.*

—Romans 10:9–10

The Ultimate Freedom

Although this is the last chapter in this book, please know that this freedom is not the least of them. In fact, this freedom is the ultimate and supreme freedom! It is freedom from sin. According to Romans 3:23–24, "All have sinned and come short of the glory of God." Sin is rebellion against God, and the wages of sin is death. When we sin, we damage ourselves and hurt others, and we dishonor God. The power of sin will hold you captive as a slave shackled in chains. It will do its best to keep you bound until death. Freedom from sin is salvation! We all need salvation and deliverance from sin. Without salvation, we are doomed with an eternity separated from God.

The Plan of Salvation

Choosing to receive Christ and salvation is the biggest and most important decision of your life. God loved us so much that while we were still sinners, Christ died for us (Romans 5:8). He was the ultimate sacrifice, and his death paid for all our past, present, and future sins. Receiving Christ is as easy as ABC (*A*—accepting Jesus into your heart, *B*—believing in your heart that God raised him from the dead, *C*—confessing that Jesus is Lord)! That is all you have to do to receive your salvation.

Salvation Is Now

Today I would like to offer you Christ. It doesn't matter if you are new to Christ or if you are backslidden and you need forgiveness.

Whatever you need, he's got it, and today is your day! If you are ready to receive Jesus Christ as your Lord and Savior by faith, you are ready to make the best decision of your life! I am so happy for you and your decision for Christ. I pray that you will open your heart and let him in. This is your opportunity to change your life for the better. All you have to do is read this simple prayer aloud and believe, and you shall be saved.

Salvation Prayer

"Lord Jesus, I repent of my sin. I accept and believe in my heart that God raised you from the dead. Today I confess and make you my Lord and Savior. Amen."

Salvation Certificate

Congratulations! You have just made the best decision of your life! I am so happy for you! I have included a certificate of salvation just for you. Please fill your certificate out and take a picture of it. Then I would love for you to share your salvation story and a picture of your certificate with me on our "Freedom for Your Soul Book

Club" Facebook page. This will help me know how many souls were won for Christ. Finally, I believe that your testimony will help win more souls for Christ as well.

If you enjoyed reading this, please leave a review on Amazon. I read every review and they help new readers discover my book. I would really appreciate that! Thanks in advance!

What's Next after Salvation

Accepting Jesus and receiving salvation is just the beginning. I would like to share two websites with you that will help you as you start your journey with Christ. The first website is www.Gotquestions.org/now-what2.html. This website will ensure that you get off to a good start by going over the following five topics:

1. Make sure you understand salvation.
2. Find a good church that teaches the Bible.
3. Set aside time each day to focus on God.
4. Develop relationships with people who can help you spiritually.
5. Be baptized.

The final website that I would like to share is www.twenty-20faith.org/gotquestions-en. This website provides six foundation-building devotions that are important pillars of our Christian faith:

1. The Biggest Decision of Your Life!
2. Give God First Place!
3. Your Best Investment!
4. You Do Have a Prayer!
5. Shine Your Light!
6. Live with Strength and Courage!

I pray that these resources will help guide you into your best life with Christ. I am so happy for you and proud of you for making the best decision of your life.

My Prayer for You

Father God, I thank you for this person, who has given their life to you or repented of their sins! I pray that you will put up a hedge of protection around them as they go through life with you. I pray that you give them the strength to overcome the obstacles, chains, and snares that the enemy will use to try to trap them. I pray that your love holds them with a warm embrace while they walk through the cold valleys of the shadow of death. I pray the blood of Jesus over them as they do the work of the kingdom of God!

When they get tired and begin to faint, renew their strength and be the wind beneath their wings as they mount up with wings as eagles. Help them to always be about the Father's business. Help them to keep you first. Direct their paths into their God-given purposes. Stick closer than a brother to them. When their faith is wavering, allow your creation to bring them back to their knees as they kneel in awe of you and your unfathomable power. Always remind them that no matter what they face, your freedom and salvation is always ready and available for them. Finally, please give them wisdom to win souls and build up the kingdom of God! These things I pray in Jesus' name. Amen!

Certificate of Salvation

FREEDOM FOR YOUR SOUL BOOK MINISTRY

CERTIFICATE OF SALVATION

THIS CERTIFICATE IS PRESENTED TO

____

IN JOYFUL CELEBRATION OF THEIR PROFESSION OF
THEIR FAITH AND ACCEPTANCE OF JESUS CHRIST AS
THEIR LORD AND SAVIOR.

TODAY, I ACCEPTED JESUS CHRIST AS MY SAVIOR. I
CONFESSED WITH MY MOUTH THE LORD JESUS AND I
BELIEVED IN MY HEART THAT GOD RAISED HIM FROM
THE DEAD, ACCORDING TO ROMANS 10:9

I AM NOW SAVED, FORGIVEN AND FREE FROM OF ALL MY
PAST, PRESENT AND FUTURE SINS.
I VOW TO LOVE GOD, HELP PEOPLE AND SERVE THE
WORLD THROUGH MY LOCAL CHURCH, AND OR
COMMUNITY.

SIGNATURE   DATE

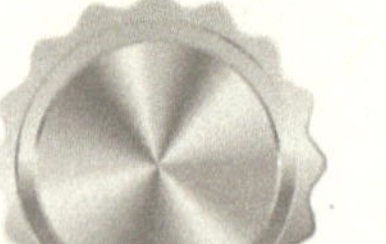

ABOUT THE AUTHOR

Terrica is a "big, bright, and beautiful" soul from the inside out. Her infectious smile and larger-than-life personality have the ability to captivate and motivate anyone she encounters, and she never meets a stranger. She is a native of Blytheville, Arkansas, where she was raised in a God-fearing home as a pastor's kid. She is the fourth of five children to Bishop James and Dr. Julia Sims. She was a loving dog mom to her beloved dog, little Ms. Blessing, for fourteen years.

She lives a Christ-centered life that is dedicated to educating, uplifting, and beautifying the world through her many God-given gifts. She is very passionate about everything that she puts her mind to. She believes that anything is possible if you just have faith and only believe!

This is Terrica's first book, and it was birth out of obedience to an assignment that God gave her. Her goal in writing this book is to help people become free and stay free from the chains that try to enslave and destroy them. Terrica is absolutely thrilled to be a new author and is overjoyed to share her book with the world. She would love to come and share with you and your organizations, churches, and schools.

For serious inquiries, please book by email at terricasims@yahoo.com or at Terrica Sims on Facebook and/or Instagram.

Terrica would like to thank everyone who will purchase her book. She prays that it blesses and transforms every area of your life. She prays that it gives you the strength to dismantle the chains off your life, and she also prays that it empowers you to take your freedom back. Her ultimate goal is that your freedom shines so brightly that others are set free by your testimony. Her final prayer is that freedom and salvation will spread like a consuming wildfire so that God will be glorified for his amazing works all over the world! Amen!